IMAGES
of America

FRANCISCAN FRIARS
COAST TO COAST

ON THE COVER: "FRANCIS, REBUILD MY CHURCH." In 1206, Francis of Assisi heard Christ speak to him from the crucifix in the small church of San Damiano and say, "Rebuild my Church." Francis immediately went to work with his own hands to rebuild that church, but before long, he, with his brothers, realized that God had lots of building in mind. Here, Br. Adrian Wewer, a noted church architect, stands with the plans in his hands for rebuilding St. Boniface Church after the Great San Francisco Earthquake of 1906. Brother Adrian had come from the Holy Cross province in Saxony and designed a number of churches, friaries, and other religious buildings across the country, from Ohio to California. The younger friar standing to Brother Adrian's right in the photograph is Josaphat Kraus, the vicar of St. Boniface. To the left of Brother Adrian is John Frederick Sperisen, with the cigar. (Paul F. Penna, Santa Rosa, California.)

IMAGES
of America

FRANCISCAN FRIARS
COAST TO COAST

Jack Clark Robinson
Foreword by Michael A. Perry

ARCADIA
PUBLISHING

Published by Arcadia Publishing
Charleston, South Carolina

Printed in the United States of America

Library of Congress Control Number: 2019943036

For all general information, please contact Arcadia Publishing:
Telephone 843-853-2070
Fax 843-853-0044
E-mail sales@arcadiapublishing.com
For customer service and orders:
Toll-Free 1-888-313-2665

Visit us on the Internet at www.arcadiapublishing.com

To the Franciscan friars
and those working with them
to bring the Gospel to life,
from coast to coast,
for hundreds of years
and into the future

CONTENTS

FOREWORD

Eleanor Roosevelt wrote, "The future belongs to those who believe in the beauty of their dreams." Her words describe the scope and depth of the life of Franciscan friars who, from coast to coast, have continuously sought to live the "beauty of their dreams."

Conveyed through archival images from six North American provinces, we learn about Franciscans coming from diverse geographical and cultural backgrounds to US shores to follow the dream they shared with the founder of their movement, St. Francis of Assisi. Their story is anything but dull, repetitive, static, or uniform. From the time of their first arrival on the shores of Florida to those of more recent immigrants who have joined Franciscan life, the Franciscan message has, fundamentally, remained the same: everyone counts; everyone is included; everyone matters to God, to the church, and to the friars.

The search to live the Franciscan dream in the United States has not been without controversies and failures. Waves of Franciscan missionaries accompanying populations fleeing violence, exclusion, poverty, and hunger in Europe demonstrated their commitment to proclaim the Gospel as a spiritually and socially liberating force, even as they struggled to be liberated from their own ideological inclinations. In their struggles, the friars resisted the temptation to close in upon themselves. Rather, they proved to be genuinely "for the people" and "with the people." This helps explain their willingness to march into war with US soldiers to provide spiritual solace; to assist in hospital wards to accompany those with contagious pathogens, to stand with those persecuted because of the color of their skin, to remain among the Navajo and other native populations in the best and worst of times, to link their lives with undocumented immigrants, and to stay with the people of the Ninth Ward in New Orleans following the catastrophic events of Hurricane Katrina.

Time and again, this book will reveal that the friars chose the higher ground, placing the content of character before personal interests, to pursue God's dream revealed to them in and through the example of St. Francis of Assisi.

—Michael Perry
Minister General of the Order of Friars Minor

ACKNOWLEDGMENTS

The photographs in this book were carefully selected by the provincial archivists of six US Franciscan Provinces of the Order of Friars Minor (OFM). Those archivists diligently preserve the stories of Franciscan friars. Without their hard work, this book would not have been possible. My thanks, gratitude, and deep appreciation go to: Denise Thuston of Sacred Heart Province; Monica Orozco, Brittany Bratcher, and Bryan Stephenson of St. Barbara Province; Ron Cooper of St. John the Baptist Province; Thomas Cole, OFM of Holy Name Province; William Stout, OFM of Assumption of the Blessed Virgin Mary Province; and finally, Brie Martin of Our Lady of Guadalupe Province, who especially went beyond the call of duty to help get things done and to help her often demanding boss—me.

Jeff Mccnab, OFM; Michael Blastic, OFM; Michael Jennrich, OFM; Kevin Schroeder, OFM; and Sr. Susan Rosenbach, S.S.S.F., the interprovincial novitiate team, generously hosted the archivists and me as we put this work together. The Academy of American Franciscan History supplied a grant to facilitate that meeting. My brother ministers provincial of the provinces portrayed here, David Gaa, James Gannon, Kevin Mullen, Thomas Nairn, and Mark Soehner, have given unwavering support.

Finally, I want to thank the Franciscan novices who have inspired and challenged me with their energy and enthusiasm for their Franciscan vocations as I have tried to share our Franciscan story with them for over 20 years.

All of the photographs in this book come from the following six sources: the Provincial Archives of Sacred Heart Province, St. Louis, Missouri (SHPA); Provincial Archives of St. John the Baptist Province, Cincinnati, Ohio (SJBPA); Provincial Archives of Holy Name Province, Butler, New Jersey (HNPA); Provincial Archives of St. Barbara Province, Santa Barbara, California (SBPA); Provincial Archives of the Assumption of the Blessed Virgin Mary Province, Burlington, Wisconsin (ABVMPA); and Provincial Archives of Our Lady of Guadalupe Province, Albuquerque, New Mexico (OLGPA).

INTRODUCTION

In 1223, Francis of Assisi and 5,000 brothers received formal Roman Catholic Church approval for their rule of life. Though Francis and his companions always referred to themselves as brothers, they have commonly come to be called friars in English to indicate that their brotherhood is a special kind of religious bond. They share the term friars with Dominicans, Augustinians, and Carmelites in the Roman Catholic Church. Collectively, the followers of St. Francis are also often called Franciscans, after their founder. Their official Latin name, Ordo Fratrum Minorum, translates to "Order of Friars Minor"; however, more accurately, it might be "Band of Little Brothers." The early friars included the word *minorum*, or "minor," in their name to indicate that they were not to be considered important, but instead to be thought "lesser ones," as they went about the world.

Their rule, based on the life that the brothers had lived together since 1209, contained the first-ever provision for the members of a Catholic religious community to go to foreign lands and serve as missionaries of the Gospel. Franciscans have always gone to faraway places as missionaries. Along the way, two Popes have divided that one community of men founded by Francis into three entities: the Order of Friars Minor (OFM); the Order of Friars Minor Conventual (OFM Conv), and the Order of Friars Minor Capuchin (OFM Cap). Though the members of these three groups put different initials after their names and are legally separate from one another, each with its own hierarchy all the way from the local friars to their three individual Ministers General in Rome, they all trace their heart and soul to the inspiration of Francis of Assisi.

In 1493, members of the Order of Friars Minor became the first Christian missionaries in the western hemisphere when they traveled with Christopher Columbus on his second voyage of discovery. Some say that they would have come in 1492, but they wanted to make sure that Columbus made it home from his first trip. In the 1500s, the kings of Spain sent Franciscan friars alongside conquistadors and colonizers to Florida, Georgia, and New Mexico. In 1712, the Franciscan friars arrived in Texas, and they got to California in 1769. Often, the Franciscan friars came into conflict with the Spanish royal authorities whom they accompanied. The friars' primary intention in coming to America was to share the Gospel of Jesus Christ with those who had never heard it before. They came first to promote the Reign of God because, in the early years, they were convinced that Christ would return once the Gospel had been shared with the last people on earth who had not had the opportunity to hear it. Though caught up in the Spanish Empire and its culture, spreading that empire was to them a secondary purpose.

In one place or another, Franciscan friars have been in what is now the United States without interruption since the 16th century. Among all groups of people to be found in this country today, including civil government, families, or associations of any sort, the only groups who can claim a longer continuous presence in the United States than Franciscan friars would be Native American tribes and nations, with whom they so often worked and with whom they still work.

Though Franciscan friars today can trace an unbroken connection back to the Spanish colonial times, their history in the United States falls into two distinct eras. The first era, with top-down colonial evangelization initially sponsored by Spanish royalty, was from the 1530s, when it began in the Southwest, until 1821, when Mexico, which at the time included present-day California and New Mexico, gained its independence from Spain. Friars from an independent Mexico remained in California and New Mexico until the 1840s. By the 1840s, great numbers of Catholic immigrants began to arrive in the United States, first from Ireland and then from other parts of Europe a short time later. Because they were often accompanied by Franciscan friars, so in the United States, the second Franciscan era overlaps the first.

The Catholic immigrants from Europe in the mid-19th century were not coming from the top of society, with military might to overpower others already present when they arrived. Instead, these Catholic immigrants arrived at the bottom of the social ladder. They were soon accompanied by many Franciscan friars, as well as other Catholic clergy and religious sisters. For along with the desire to spread the Gospel to those who had never heard it, Francis of Assisi had also instilled in his followers a desire to be with those on the margins, especially the poor and despised of the world. The most despised people of his day were lepers. Just before he died, Francis of Assisi wrote in his *Testament*, his most self-reflective writing, that his own conversion to a fuller, deeper understanding of the Gospel of Jesus Christ came to him when he went among lepers. Franciscan friars have long heard and heeded the call to go to the lepers of their day, those on the margins of society.

Catholic immigrants arriving in the United States from 1850 to 1900 were indeed "lepers," people on the margins. These immigrants generally arrived after being pushed to emigrate by events in Europe, such as the potato famine in Ireland in the 1840s and the continent-wide social upheavals of 1848. Social upheaval continued through the 1870s, with the German Kulturkampf, the movement to establish the dominance of Prussian culture over the entire German Empire, and the Italian Risorgimento, the unification of the Italian states into the Kingdom of Italy. When Catholic immigrants arrived, they were not welcomed by the Protestant majority who had already firmly established themselves throughout the United States east of the Mississippi River. In the 1850s, anti-Catholic mobs rioted in the streets, setting fire to Roman Catholic neighborhoods in Philadelphia, New York, Boston, Cincinnati, and Louisville. In Philadelphia, New York, and Boston, the despised Roman Catholics were mostly Irish, but in Cincinnati and Louisville, they were largely immigrants from German-speaking lands. Franciscan friars were among those German-speaking Catholics.

Language and geography played a large part in where immigrants eventually settled across the Eastern United States in the 19th century. The states that had been part of the original 13 English colonies were well-settled and dominated by English speakers. Irish immigrants, coming from a land that had endured English colonization for hundreds of years, had the advantage of knowing English and being able to find a place, a very low place, in the society of the Eastern Seaboard. When German-speaking immigrants arrived in the 1850s, they wanted land for farming and a place where they could speak German. To get those things, they crossed the Appalachian Mountains and made their way down the Ohio River and along the Mississippi River, as well as going north to the Great Lakes. Their settlements formed a "German triangle," and its boundaries were marked by the three cities of Cincinnati, St. Louis, and Milwaukee. Repeatedly, Roman Catholic bishops on this frontier sought out German-speaking priests and religious sisters to serve the ever-growing numbers of immigrants who came to their dioceses.

Two Provinces of the Order of Friars Minor, Sacred Heart Province headquartered in St. Louis and St. John the Baptist Province headquartered in Cincinnati, came about as a direct result of this first wave of German immigration in the 1850s. German Franciscan immigration initially remained steady through the 1850s and 1860s but turned into a torrent in the 1870s, when Otto von Bismarck, the Protestant Prussian chancellor of Germany, ordered all members of Roman Catholic religious communities to disband or leave the country in 1875 as part of the Kulturkampf. That forced exodus of German-speaking Roman Catholic religious would change the face of Roman Catholicism in the United States. The diocesan priesthood in the United States in the 19th century came largely from Irish immigrants and the sons of Irish immigrants; however, there were also pockets of French-speaking immigrant priests in New Mexico and elsewhere. But the accent of US religious communities from the 1870s to World War I was German, as Bismarck sought to rid the German Empire of Roman Catholic religious communities.

The 1870s arrival of German-speaking Franciscan friars had a great impact on the founding of both Sacred Heart and Holy Name Provinces. Polish-speaking immigrants began arriving in large numbers in the 1880s, and once again, language and geography played a role in where they decided to settle. The farmland of Ohio, Illinois, Indiana, Missouri, and Kansas was already largely occupied by German-speaking immigrants and their descendants, so the Polish-speakers, went north, and the Polish-speaking Province of the Assumption of the Blessed Virgin Mary would eventually emerge in Wisconsin. Between 1890 and 1920, a large influx of Italian immigrants, with their own unique need for ministry, came to East Coast cities, leading to the establishment of Immaculate Conception Province of the Order of Friars Minor in 1910.

This book began as an initiative of the archivists of the six included provinces to share their provinces' stories with each other as those provinces unite. Immaculate Conception Province chose not to be part of that unification nor to participate in preparation of this book.

The last two provinces founded in the western United States came about a bit differently from the immigrant pattern. The very last remnant of the colonial Franciscan effort in the United States was in Santa Barbara, California. By 1885, the friars there and their mission had fallen on such hard times that the minister general of the order directed that the mission and its friars become part of the Sacred Heart Province, which, by that time, was established in St. Louis, Missouri. Likewise, the origins of Our Lady of Guadalupe Province lie in the desire of St. Katharine Drexel to found a mission school among the Navajo Indians in the Southwest. She persuaded Franciscan friars from Cincinnati to send missionaries to the Navajo Reservation, and from there, they spread to other parts of Arizona and New Mexico, overlapping the missions of Sacred Heart and then St. Barbara Province at times.

The images in this book will attempt to tell some of the story of Franciscans, who came both to spread the Gospel and serve European immigrants in the 1800s, and their growth into six provinces, or autonomous units, of the worldwide Order of Friars Minor. These six provinces are only part of the Franciscan story in the United States, but even this incomplete story of Franciscans in the United States stretches from the Atlantic to the Pacific and from the Great Lakes to the Gulf of Mexico—truly coast to coast. The thousands of friars who belonged to these provinces over the last 170 years literally touched the lives of millions of Roman Catholics and others. One book cannot tell their story, but it can invite reflection on some of what they have done and encourage readers to look further into this amazing story of Franciscan friars from coast to coast.

One

SACRED HEART PROVINCE

Sacred Heart Province would emerge as the first Franciscan Province in the United States in 1879 because, in the late 1850s, Gregor Janknecht had the courage to send nine friars from Saxony to the missions of far-off Illinois on what was then the western frontier of the United States. Those sent included seven members of the First Order, who, under the Recollect understanding of the Franciscan rule, were not able to touch money, and two tertiary brothers, who could handle the money. Among them were Sevace Altmicks, the first president of St. Francis College, later Quincy University, and Edmund Wilde, who became Brother Herman and outlived the eight others, dying as a friar in 1908.

Gregor Janknecht also had the foresight to prepare for the Prussian Kulturkampf. When laws forbidding Roman Catholic religious life went into effect in May 1875, Gregor Janknecht took action to preserve the community. He sent over 100 students, young friars, professors, and leaders to the United States on one ship! With that sudden influx of friars, the slow, steady growth of the community exploded into the new Province of the Most Sacred Heart of Jesus on April 26, 1879. Fledgling missions in Illinois, Missouri, Ohio, Tennessee, and Wisconsin became firmly established. In 1885, they expanded to California and, in 1894, took responsibility for Polish friars in Wisconsin. By 1900, friars, once part of the province, were missionaries in China; in 1942, friars went to the Amazon basin of Brazil; and in 1977, they traveled to Zaire.

FOUNDING FRIAR, GREGOR JANKNECHT. In 1858, Bishop Henry Damian Juncker of Alton, Illinois, knocked on the friary door of Gregor Janknecht, the 28-year-old minister provincial of the Holy Cross Province. Holy Cross Province located in Westphalia, part of the Duchy of Saxony, was itself struggling to come back to life from a severe decline after all of the religious, social, and political turmoil in Europe during the 1840s and 1850s. To Bishop Juncker's great surprise, Janknecht himself answered the door of the friary, then sat with the bishop, and heard him delineate the great need for German-speaking priests to minister among immigrants in his newly established diocese. To the bishop's delight, Janknecht agreed to send friars to help, and thus, the first steps were taken for the founding of Sacred Heart Province. Gregor Janknecht helped found not only the Sacred Heart Province but also a province in Brazil, served as a general definitor of the worldwide Order of Friars Minor, and promoted reform of the Franciscans in Ireland. (SHPA.)

A St. Louis Heart. St. Anthony Church and Friary in the heart of an old German neighborhood called Dutchtown, a corruption of *Deutsch*, the German language word for German, has been a Franciscan landmark in St. Louis for nearly 90 years. From this location, not only have friars served the local parish and school, but these buildings have also housed the administrative offices and archives of the province, as well as a residence where friars have rested when home from foreign missions, lived in semiretirement, and gone forth to serve other institutions, including hospitals and jails in the St. Louis area. Dedicated in 1932, the motherhouse has seen countless meetings of the Provincial Definitorium and probably nearly every other group of friars ever asked by the province to form a committee or take up a special task. Secular Franciscans have also met here and been a big part of the life of the Franciscans of Sacred Heart Province. (SHPA.)

CENTENNIAL PROCESSION. In 1958, the friars and the people of surrounding Dutchtown celebrated the 100th anniversary of the coming of Franciscan friars from Saxony to the Midwest of the United States with a procession through neighborhood streets. By this time, the handful of immigrant friars who first came to Teutopolis, in the then Diocese of Alton, now Springfield, Illinois, had become hundreds of friars, both clerics and lay, who served not only in Illinois and Missouri but also throughout the Midwest and as far away as Brazil, having at one time also had a number of missions in China. The membership of the province included distinguished educators and scholars—both at Quincy College and elsewhere—preachers, spiritual directors, pastors, and pastoral ministers, who served big city parishes in Chicago and St. Louis, as well as small farm communities in Nebraska. (SHPA.)

THE CORD'S CONTINUITY AND CHANGE.
The cord around the waist of a friar in
his habit not only holds the habit in
place but also symbolizes an unbroken
connection of friars from one generation
to the next through the ages. Here,
Br. William Tewes shows how cords
were woven for centuries before Br.
Ignatius Zweisler and others developed
a cord-making machine. (SHPA.)

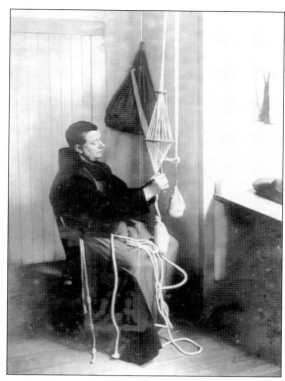

SANDAL-SHOD FOOTSTEPS. Like the
cord around the waist, sandals have
been a hallmark of Franciscan dress
since the 13th century. The fraternity
cobbler was long an important part
of helping friars be friars. (SHPA.)

CLOTHING ACCORDING TO COLD CLIMATES. The friars have always been called to simple clothes, but not without consideration of the climate where they live. These novices with shorn heads certainly appreciated their heavy woolen, winter mantles (cloaks). (SHPA.)

CLOTHING ACCORDING TO WARM CLIMATES. Though known for their simple brown habits, the friars have long made the sensible change to white habits, such as those worn here, to deal with tropical sunshine and heat. Pictured from left to right, Frs. Jude Prost, James Ryan, Severin Nelles, and Juniper Freitag were the first friars to go from the United States to the Santarem Prelature in Brazil in 1943. (SHPA.)

NONTRADITIONAL CLOTHES. Franciscan friars served as chaplains to those in the US military during all major 20th-century foreign conflicts. Posing in his tent near the front lines of fighting, Aidan Potter, with his helmet at the ready, served as an Army chaplain during World War II. (SHPA.)

SOME GAVE ALL. During World War II, 26 friars of Sacred Heart Province served as military chaplains. Myles O'Toole, ever popular with his men, died on Luzon Island after being struck by shrapnel on January 19, 1945. (SHPA.)

PREPARED FOR SERVICE. Friars who gave themselves totally in the service of the Gospel and others did so after following a call from God through years of training. Their formation began as high school students at St. Joseph Seminary, Westmont, Illinois, where participation in regular religious exercises instilled in them reverence and faith. (SHPA.)

PLACES OF PREPARATION. Cardinal Mundelein, archbishop of Chicago, blessed the St. Joseph Franciscan seminary in 1927. For many years, the seminary served as the first place of studies for young men preparing to become friars in Sacred Heart Province. (SHPA.)

TEUTOPOLIS, WHERE THINGS BEGAN. The first ministry of the friars who came from Saxony to the United States in the 1858 was in Teutopolis, Illinois. There, they welcomed young men seeking to become Franciscan friars or diocesan priests. Here, a group of seminarians, either on their way to or from the seminary, stood at the Teutopolis train station around the turn of the 20th century. (SHPA.)

BEHIND THE TEUTOPOLIS WALLS. From 1860 until 1967, St. Francis Friary in Teutopolis served as the Sacred Heart provincial novitiate. For a year-and-a-day, novices lived an intense life of regulated prayer, enclosed within the sacred space of the novitiate, only rarely leaving the grounds. So in the 1920s, Athanasius Steck (left), Theodore Worm (center), and their companion enjoyed a pleasant afternoon but stayed "behind the wall." (SHPA.)

Philosophy Studies. After the minor seminary, future Franciscan friars training to be priests undertook the study of philosophy. Under the watchful eye of Victor Hoffman, philosophy students at Our Lady of the Angels Seminary in West Park, Ohio, in 1913 intently prepared for the future study of theology. (SHPA.)

Music for Heart and Soul. A 1958 photograph shows young friars engaged in music practice at St. Joseph College and Seminary in Teutopolis, Illinois. Sacred music was an important part of the training of young friars, who would chant psalms and other liturgical passages both inside the community and in public religious services. (SHPA.)

PRIVATE PREPARATION. Not all the preparation for Franciscan ministry was done in groups. A vital element of that preparation was quiet prayer and meditation, as exemplified by these friars kneeling in prayer before the Blessed Sacrament at St. Joseph Seminary in Westmont, Illinois, around 1934. (SHPA.)

ANOTHER KIND OF STUDY. Franciscan brothers with a wide variety of talents put their gifts to use in many different ways to support the proclamation of the Gospel. Young friars at St. Paschal Brothers' School made furniture for use throughout the province. (SHPA.)

ORDINATIONS IN 1938. With the passing of years, formation at Teutopolis led to the ordination of many Franciscan friars who would go on to serve throughout Sacred Heart Province and its far-flung missions. Anticipation and excitement showed on the faces of these young men on their way to be ordained priests. (SHPA.)

ORDINATIONS IN 1946. One of the most important keepsakes of families and friends of the newly ordained priests and deacons, as well as for the friar himself, was a picture of that young friar with his ordination classmates and the ordaining bishop. (SHPA.)

A First Blessing. The blessings given by young priests soon after their ordination have always been considered special moments of ministry and grace. In this photograph, Dismas Bonner, who went on to be minister provincial of Sacred Heart Province, bestows a first blessing on a fellow friar. (SHPA.)

A Different First Blessing. Sacred Heart Province contributed Richard Duffy to the African Vicariate, formed in 1981 by friars from all over the world. Those friars came together to extend the Franciscan proclamation of the Gospel to that continent in a new, intercultural way. Richard is pictured here giving his first blessing to new parishioners in Africa. (SHPA.)

MISSIONS WERE NOT ALL NEW. Ordoric Derenthal served as an early Franciscan missionary among the Menominee Indians in Keshena, Wisconsin, in 1885. Beyond fleeing the Kulturkampf, the opportunity to minister with Native Americans was a strong draw for some of the first friars who came from Saxony to America. (SHPA.)

FRANCISCANS EMBRACED MISSION LIFE. The first pioneer work among Native Americans in Minnesota, Wisconsin, and Michigan began before the province was formed. In this 1923 photograph, one of the friars serving among Native Americans had so entered into the life of the people he served that he was given a native name by the people—Mino-gijig. He is posed here between Bi-mia-kwash (left) and Ma-kwa-ni-i-gons (right). (SHPA.)

OLD AND NEW MISSIONS. The Spanish colonial missions in San Antonio, Texas, were founded by Franciscan friars in the early 1700s. Friars of Sacred Heart Province began to serve them in the 1930s. Pictured while on a visit to present a parish mission, John Joseph Brogger stands in front of the famous Rose Window of Mission San Jose. (SHPA.)

JUNIPERO SERRA CONNECTION. Sacred Heart Province has a deep connection to the Spanish colonial missions of California as well as Texas. From 1885 until 1915, the Franciscans of California, initially only at Santa Barbara but eventually expanding throughout the state, were part of Sacred Heart Province. In St. Francis Church in Teutopolis, a stained-glass window recalls St. Junipero Serra. (SHPA.)

ORDINATION AT ST. FRANCIS CHURCH. This 1946 photograph, taken from the choir loft, of the ordination of young friars in St. Francis Church in Teutopolis, Illinois, offers a glimpse of the rich ornamentation arising from Franciscan devotion to the ceremonies of the church. (SHPA.)

ONCE ORDAINED, GO FORTH INTO THE WORLD. As their missions stretched over time from Alaska and Hawaii to Brazil, friars traveled far from Teutopolis. In Brazil, this friar priest offered God's mercy to some very young penitents along the Amazon and Tapajos Rivers, where friars said Mass, performed marriages, baptized the young, anointed the sick, and heard confessions, as seen here in 1944. (SHPA.)

OAK BROOK "MISSIONS." The procession of lay retreatants was a standard feature of lay retreats conducted by the friars. Here, the procession came from a replica chapel of Our Lady of the Angels in Assisi at the St. Francis retreat house in Oak Brook, Illinois, built in 1926. (SHPA.)

QUINCY UNIVERSITY. From the 1850s, the province evangelized by providing higher education with the aim of ensuring classical and commercial programs were available both for young men aspiring to the Franciscan Order and for lay students. Seen here, as it stood in 1892 while still called St. Francis Solanus College in Quincy, Illinois, is one school built for that purpose and later renamed Quincy College and then Quincy University. (SHPA.)

COMMITMENT AND CHANGE. Friars from Saxony arrived in 1858, and 150 years later, the friars of Sacred Heart Province remained a vital force for good and for the proclamation of the Gospel, as they stretched across the United States' midsection from Wisconsin to Texas and reached out to Alaska, Brazil, and Vietnam. They were often very different from one another, with different gifts and talents, as well as many different ideas about how to follow the call of the Gospel. But they continued to be empowered by their commitment through the years to the same vows: obedience, poverty, and chastity. Here, a group of friars in St. Anthony Church in St. Louis marked the 150th anniversary of the arrival of those early friars by renewing their vows. (SHPA.)

Two

St. John the Baptist Province

St. John the Baptist Province emerged from the mid-19th-century flood of German immigrants into the Ohio Valley. German immigrants, both Catholic and Protestant, came down the Ohio River, stopped in Cincinnati, and chose to stay. They faced prejudice and rejection from English-speaking neighbors, including riots and bloodshed in the 1850s. The first German Catholic settlement was a neighborhood called "Over-the-Rhine," which was located across a canal and outside the city limits of Cincinnati. There Tyrolese Franciscans settled among them.

The Tyrol, from which they came, overlaps western Austria, Eastern Switzerland, and North Central Italy. The Tyrol never became part of the German Empire, and thus, they never suffered the Kulturkampf expulsion of Roman Catholic religious communities. So St. John the Baptist Custody, and after 1885 St. John the Baptist Province, grew slowly, as there was never a mass migration of friars from Tyrol to the United States.

Like Franciscan friars elsewhere, those of St. John the Baptist took up ministry in many frontier parishes, responding to the call of bishops and the needs of the immigrant church. Initially, all parish ministry among urban immigrant communities was also ministry involving issues of peace, justice, and the survival of struggling people on the margins. As popular evangelizers, the friars of St. John the Baptist produced magazines, the mass media of the day. Eventually, their mission spirit also led to a deep commitment to work among Native Americans in the Southwest.

29

FOUNDING FRIAR, OTTO JAIR. St. John the Baptist Province began in 1844 when Franciscans from St. Leopold Province in Tyrol arrived in Cincinnati. They were responding to calls for German-speaking priests to serve Catholic immigrants in the same way a few years later friars from Holy Cross Province in Saxony would go to Illinois. The number of friars grew slowly with gradual immigration by Tyrolese friars, some of whom did return to Europe. In 1854 and 1857, the provincial chapter of St. Leopold Province ordered all of the Cincinnati missionaries to return home. Otto Jair was head of the mission in Cincinnati at the time. He and the friars with him saw the need for their ministry in Ohio, and they did not want to leave. Otto Jair turned to Cincinnati's Archbishop John Baptist Purcell for help. Together, they negotiated an arrangement with the general administration of the Order of Friars Minor in Rome, which allowed the friars in Cincinnati to become a custody in 1859, an autonomous unit of the order. (SJBPA.)

First Parish, St. John's. Friars came from the Tyrol to Cincinnati responding to Bishop Purcell's call for ministry among German-speaking immigrants. As the bishop sought to establish and regularize that ministry, the friars were asked to serve in parishes. The friars served at St. John's, officially St. John the Baptist, from 1846 until the parish closed in 1969. (SJBPA.)

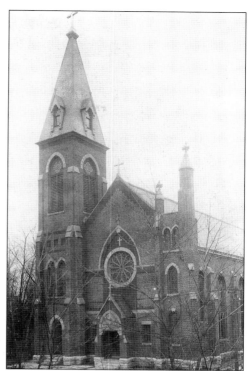

The Motherhouse. Though service in parishes that belonged to dioceses where they were located was very much a part of the life of 19th-century Franciscans, religious life demanded that they have places set apart for their own communal activities, like a motherhouse. St. Francis Seraph has served both as a motherhouse and parish setting since the 1850s. (SJBPA.)

COLLEGIUM FRANCISCANUM. To become a Franciscan required formation, both intellectual and spiritual. The first place that the Franciscans in Cincinnati established for that purpose was their college in 1858. Franciscans in the United States were among the first to establish minor seminaries, where teenage boys lived in a boarding school setting while studying to enter Franciscan life and ministry. (SJBPA.)

ST. FRANCIS SERAPH MINOR SEMINARY. In the 1920s, the number of youth from among the sons and grandsons of immigrants coming to join the Franciscans was such that a new minor seminary was built to accommodate their numbers in Mount Healthy, a neighborhood on the edge of Cincinnati. Many young men received a well-rounded high school education there until the seminary closed in 1980. (SJBPA.)

St. Anthony Shrine. The Shrine and Friary of St. Anthony of Padua in the Mount Airy neighborhood of Cincinnati, shown here under construction, has been an important focus of Franciscan life and formation since 1888. For generations, the life of Franciscan friars officially began as they "took the habit of probation" here as novices. (SJBPA.)

Soon-to-Be Novices Arrive. Franciscan friars along with the whole country experienced a baby boom following World War II. Inspired by older brothers, uncles, and fathers who had served their country, the young men shown here were part of an unprecedented growth of Franciscans wanting to serve God in the United States in the 1950s as they arrived to begin their novitiate year at St. Anthony Friary. (SJBPA.)

DUNS SCOTUS COLLEGE. Named for a famous 13th-century Franciscan philosopher, Duns Scotus College in Detroit served as the residence and place of the study of philosophy, the undergraduate degree goal of young friars who completed the novitiate with a desire to be ordained priests. (SJBPA.)

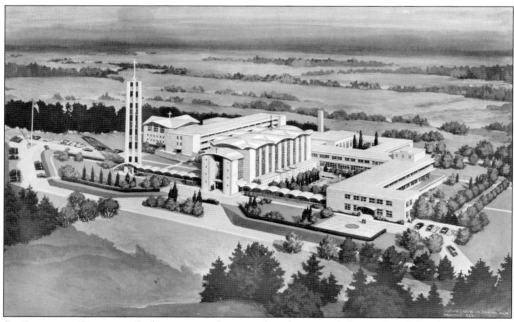

ST. LEONARD COLLEGE. Ordination to the priesthood required the study of theology upon the completion of philosophy studies. Built in the 1950s and named for a famous Franciscan preacher, St. Leonard of Port Maurice, the college outside of Dayton, Ohio, provided a place for Franciscans of St. John the Baptist Province to complete their initial formation. (SJBPA.)

THE BROTHERS' SCHOOL. For Franciscan friars not seeking ordination to the priesthood, formation also continued after novitiate in the Brothers' School, which prepared friars in a dozen different ways, including plumbing, electrical work, carpentry, clerical work, tailoring, sandal-making, and cooking. Through the 1960s and 1970s, that school was in Oldenburg, Indiana. (SJBPA.)

ST. CLEMENT CHURCH. Upon the completion of initial formation, the life of a Franciscan friar was dedicated to prayer and service while living in fraternity. Historically, that service largely revolved around parishes, such as St. Clement in St. Bernard, Ohio. Over the years, dozens of young men were inspired by the friars at St. Clement to seek to become friars, too. (SJBPA.)

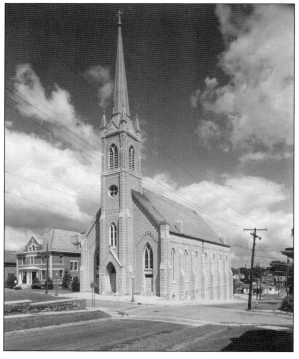

ROGER BACON HIGH SCHOOL.
Begun as a boys' high school in 1928, Roger Bacon, named for a medieval Franciscan scholar, went coeducational in 1984. Initially, the faculty was largely made up of friars, who lived in the same community as the friars working in St. Clement Parish next door. Over the years, lay teachers, including women, eventually outnumbered the friars on the faculty. (SJBPA.)

ST. MARY, BLOOMINGTON, ILLINOIS.
As the Franciscans answered the call to serve across the Midwest, they took up the administration of St. Mary Parish in 1881, where 128 different friars served the people of the parish until ministry there was returned to the Diocese of Peoria in 2016. (SJBPA.)

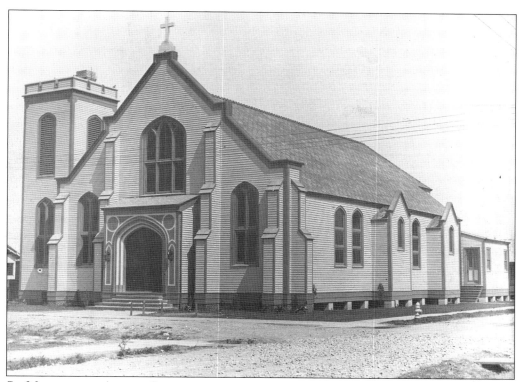

St. Mary of the Angels. In 2005, when Hurricane Katrina devastated the Ninth Ward of New Orleans, the friars had already been there at St. Mary of the Angels parish for 80 years. Three friars and dozens of parishioners were trapped by floodwaters in the parish school, but after several days, they were rescued by helicopter shuttles. (SJBPA.)

Our Lady of Good Harbor. The friars went to those on the margins of society, though not everyone agreed with their ideals. In 1963, as Chris Schneider and the friars prepared for the racial integration of Our Lady of Good Harbor School in Buras, Louisiana, the school was bombed. No one was harmed by the bombing, and integration at the school continued. (SJBPA.)

BEYOND PARISH WALLS. Friars Club began as an effort in 1908 to provide a place for building character and physical health for young men of limited means, often newly arrived from rural Appalachia and not Roman Catholic. This facility was followed by others at different Cincinnati locations. The latest facility opened in 2014 near Roger Bacon High School to serve both boys and girls. (SJBPA.)

BEYOND BORDERS. In 1898, Arizona and New Mexico were territories, not states, so when Franciscan friars Placidus Buerger (standing), Juvenal Schnorbus (left), and Anselm Weber (right) went to St. Michaels, Arizona, they were "on the margins." The friars in the Southwest continued to be part of St. John the Baptist Province until 1985, and the chapter on Our Lady of Guadalupe Province introduces that story. (SJBPA.)

BEYOND BORDERS, ARIZONA. St. Katharine Drexel (left) often visited the Southwest Franciscan missions that she helped get started. Here, at Chinle, Arizona, in 1927, she and Mother M. Francis McCann visit with, from left to right, Friar Emanuel Trockur, Friar Jerome Hesse, interpreter John Foley of Chinle, Friar Clementine Wottle, and Navajo interpreters Dan Kinlichini of Keams Canyon and Chic Sandoval of Lukachukai. (OLGPA.)

CHINA, REMBERT KOWALSKI. After serving as a missionary in New Mexico, Rembert Kowalski went to China. He was named to succeed Bishop Sylvester Espelage, OFM; but he was imprisoned by the Japanese who had overrun China. Kowalski was ordained bishop while in the Japanese concentration camp. After his release, he was imprisoned by Communists for two years and repatriated to the United States in 1953. (SJBPA.)

JAPAN, BERNARDINE SCHNEIDER. Though China was closed to US missionaries, they still wanted to go to Asia. Outstanding among them was Bernardine Schneider who spent 50 years working on the translation of the Christian scriptures into the Japanese language, resulting in the 2011 publication of a critical edition Japanese-language Bible. (SJBPA.)

PHILIPPINES, CULTIVATING. Friars of St. John the Baptist also went to the Philippines when they could no longer go to China. Their ministry there, with that of friars of St. Barbara and Assumption Provinces, included reinforcing and cultivating the faith first planted by Spanish Franciscans 400 years ago. (SJBPA.)

PHILIPPINES, SERVICE. The missions in the Philippines included lots of direct ministry to the people. Here, Fr. Elwin Harrington celebrated the sacrament of reconciliation with a parishioner. This early-1960s photograph shows the typical layout of furniture for celebrating the sacrament at that time. (SJBPA.)

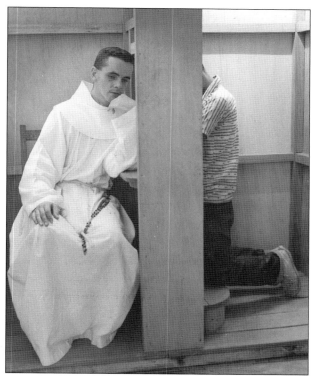

PHILIPPINES, TEACHING. The US Franciscans did lots of faith formation, such as in the catechism classed pictured here, and training young men to be friars. They were part of the founding of Our Lady of the Angels Seminary in Quezon City, and several friars of St. John the Baptist Province joined the newly formed Province of San Pedro Bautista in 1983. (SJBPA.)

VALENTINE SCHAAF, MINISTER GENERAL. Entering the friars in 1901 and ordained eight years later, Valentine Schaaf was noted from his youth for his intellectual ability and work ethic. He studied canon law and served on the theology faculty of the Catholic University of America before being elected to the General Definitorium of the Order of Friars Minor in 1939. Once the United States entered World War II against the Axis powers of Japan, Germany, and Italy, his American origins restricted his ability to travel, but he continued to serve on the General Definitorium in Rome. On the feast of St. Bonaventure in July 1945, with the Pacific war still underway and with the unsettled conditions in postwar Europe, Pope Pius XII appointed him minister general of the order in lieu of any attempt to hold a general chapter. Among his accomplishments in the short time before he died on December 1, 1946, was the consolidation of 18 small Italian provinces and the promotion of missionary activity to heal the wounds of war. (SJBPA.)

WRITER MURRAY BODO.
One of the most influential Franciscan writers in the United States, Murray Bodo wrote *The Journey and the Dream*. Selling over 227,000 copies and translated into eight languages, the book inspired many religious vocations. A 40th anniversary edition was published in 2012. (SJBPA.)

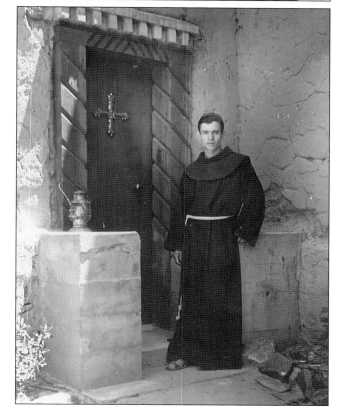

WRITER ANGELICO CHAVEZ.
Born in New Mexico in 1910, Angelico Chavez traveled east for Franciscan formation, excelling as a writer, artist, and poet. Returning to New Mexico for ordination and ministry, he later served as a military chaplain, making beachhead landings during World War II. Back home, he wrote local history and organized the archives of the Archdiocese of Santa Fe. The State History Library of New Mexico is named for him. (SJBPA.)

THE HOLY FAMILY.

St. Anthony's Messenger.

. . . ORGAN OF . . .

THE THIRD ORDER OF ST. FRANCIS,

AND DEVOTED TO

THE INTERESTS OF THE HOLY FAMILY ASSOCIATION.

VOLUME I.

JUNE 1893—1894.

PUBLISHED BY THE FRANCISCAN FATHERS,

CINCINNATI, OHIO.

ST. ANTHONY MESSENGER. The friars sought to extend the reach of their proclamation of the Gospel. In 1893, they began to publish the *St. Anthony Messenger* as a companion in English to the German *St. Franciscus Bote*, or *St. Francis Messenger*. Eventually, the *St. Anthony Messenger* had more subscribers than any other Catholic family publication in the United States. The provincial commitment to communications and media has continued for over 125 years, with various other resources, such as *Catholic Update* and *Homily Helps*, produced as paper resources, and "Saint of the Day" and various meditations, becoming part of the electronic presence of the friars on the Internet. In 2011, in recognition of the diversity of forms of communication by then in use, the entire operation was renamed Franciscan Media in place of St. Anthony Messenger Press. (SJBPA.)

WRITER RUDOLPH DILONG. A Slovak friar who lived from 1905 to 1986, he endured many of the tragedies of the 20th century. He turned those experiences into poetry, prose, novels, and plays. After World War II, he moved first to Argentina and, in the 1960s, to the United States, all along capturing the nostalgia and faith of his fellow immigrant Slovaks. He spent his Franciscan life in Holy Savior Vice Province, which became part of St. John the Baptist Province in 2000. (SJBPA.)

SERVICE TO OTHERS, CHAPLAINS. Over a dozen friars of St. John the Baptist Province served as chaplains under fire in US military forces. The most famous is Herman Felthoeler, one of the first casualties of the Korean Conflict. He chose to stay behind and minister to the injured and dying while the rest of his unit escaped a Communist attack. (SJBPA.)

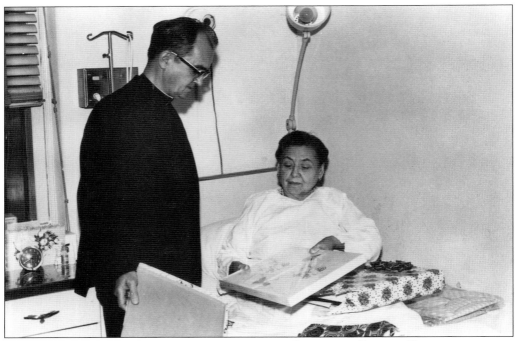

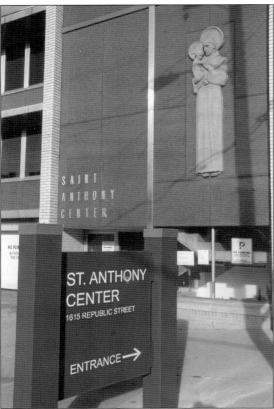

SERVICE TO OTHERS, CARVILLE.
From 1894 until 1999, the primary
care center in the continental
United States for those diagnosed
with Hansen's Disease (leprosy)
was located in Carville, Louisiana.
Alcuin Kammer began ministry there
in 1959, followed by Senan Kelly in
1961, Jerome Kircher in 1971, pictured
here with a patient, and Reynolds
Garland in 1983, who remained until
after the facility closed. (SJBPA.)

SERVICE TO OTHERS, REPURPOSING.
The Over-the-Rhine neighborhood
of Cincinnati has been friar territory
since the 1840s. The St. Anthony
Messenger Press, and then Franciscan
Media, formed and remains a large
Franciscan presence there. Recently,
more direct ministries have grown up
here, too, including Foot Care for the
Soul, Haircuts from the Heart, and St.
Mother Teresa Dining Room. (SJBPA.)

Three

HOLY NAME PROVINCE

Holy Name Province resulted from three waves of immigration bringing about two provinces. The Province of the Most Holy Name of Jesus was established in 1901, and the Province of the Immaculate Conception of the Blessed Virgin Mary came into being in 1910. Italian Franciscan friars, led by Pamfilo da Magliano, arrived in Upstate New York in 1855 and founded Immaculate Conception Custody and a school under the patronage of St. Bonaventure. They taught Irish students, and some joined the community. Those students came from the large wave of Irish immigrants of the 1840s and 1850s.

In the 1870s, a wave of immigrant Franciscan friars fleeing the Kulturkampf from a small province in Fulda established a second East Coast community of friars in Paterson, New Jersey. One of those Kulturkampf immigrants, Aloysius Lauer, returned to Europe when conditions improved in the German Empire. In the 1890s, he became minister general of the Order of Friars Minor.

Also in the 1890s, a massive wave of Italian immigrants brought both new friars and new needs for ministry. Lauer sent a friar to sort the complicated situation. David Fleming, Lauer's successor, organized the friars into two groups. Immaculate Conception Custody remained Italian and would provide parochial ministry to Italian immigrants. The ethnic Irish friars from Immaculate Conception Custody and German friars were combined into a new province, Holy Name, and continued ministry at St. Bonaventure College, as well as with the rapidly expanding Catholic population of New York and New Jersey.

FOUNDING FRIAR, PAMFILO DA MAGLIANO. Bishop John Timon of Buffalo asked Pope Pius IX for help to found a seminary in Western New York. The pope sent him to the minister general of the Franciscans, who sent him to the Irish Franciscan college of St. Isadore in Rome, where Pamfilo da Magliano, an Italian friar, had been teaching for three years. With knowledge of English and training in philosophy and theology, he was a perfect choice. Three friars accompanied Pamfilo, and with the pope's blessing, the four of them left for the United States. Bishop Timon had the promise of $5,000 and 200 acres of land from Nicholas Devereux, a wealthy Catholic businessman. On that land, St. Bonaventure College in Allegany, New York, was built. Pamfilo served as the local Franciscan guardian, custos, and president of the college for 12 years. He also helped found the Allegany, New York, Joliet, Illinois, and Rochester, Minnesota, congregations of Franciscan sisters. In 1867, he returned to Italy and worked as a scholar of Franciscan history, dying in Rome in 1875. (HNPA.)

THE ORIGINS, ST. BONAVENTURE COLLEGE. With four friars from Italy forming the core community of faculty and staff, St. Bonaventure College attracted Irish students seeking a higher education in the western section of Upstate New York. With financial support from Nicholas Devereux, the first structure, 60 by 45 feet and three stories high, was built by 1860 at a cost of $8,000, and served as friary, college, and seminary. An 1860 advertisement for the college stated, "St. Bonaventure's College, Allegany, Cattaraugus County, New York. This institution is situated near the Allegany River, within a short distance of the Allegany and Olean Stations, on the New York and Erie Railroad. The scholastic year is from the first of September to the first of July. Terms: Tuition, Board, Washing, and Mending, per annum, to be paid half-yearly in advance . . . $130.00. Modern languages and music form extra charge. Pamfilo da Magliano, O.S.F., President." (HNPA.)

FROM GERMAN LANDS. In May 1875, the anti-Catholic German laws put into effect by Otto von Bismarck meant that the only way members of religious communities could continue their religious life was to leave the German Empire. Six friars emigrated from Thuringia and Frauenberg in Fulda, Hesse, Germany, pictured here, to keep the province alive. (HNPA.)

TO AMERICAN SHORES. In 1876, the archbishop of Newark offered the Fulda friars St. Bonaventure Monastery in Paterson, New Jersey. It was reminiscent of German monasteries because it had been built by German Carmelites. (HNPA.)

FRANCIS KOCH. One of the great heroes of religious life and priestly ministry forced to come to the United States by the Kulturkampf, "the Beloved Mendicant," as Francis Koch was known, was a great promoter of the Catholic Church Extension Society. He built churches and founded parishes in New York, New Jersey, and Colorado. He developed six missions in the area of Croghan, New York, and four missions from Mohawk Hill, and it is said 20 missions in Colorado. After serving on the first provincial council when Holy Name Province was formed in 1901, Francis returned to Fulda in retirement, but his retirement only lasted a year before he returned to New Jersey to establish St. Anthony Parish in Butler, as well as the large friary there where he died on February 5, 1920, at the age of 77. (HNPA.)

LEO HEINRICHS. Francis Koch built St. Elizabeth Church in Denver, Colorado, to serve Catholics following the railroad and expanding commercial development to the foothills of the Rocky Mountains. By 1908, economic growth brought all sorts of people to Denver, including a Sicilian anarchist who shot and killed Leo Heinrichs, whom he did not know, because "priests are all against the workingman," as he told reporters. (HNPA.)

ST. JOSEPH SERAPHIC SEMINARY. Part of the still-expanding network of high school and junior college seminaries across the United States when dedicated in 1911, St. Joseph Seminary served as the training ground for generations of Franciscan friars. Besides their educational and formation duties, the faculty also served many nearby parishes. (HNPA.)

DIOCESAN ORDINATIONS. From the beginning of St. Bonaventure College, the friars provided seminary education for men studying for the diocesan priesthood, such as those being ordained here. Eventually, Christ the King Seminary grew out of its beginnings at St. Bonaventure to serve the dioceses of New York State and others in the Northeast. (HNPA.)

NORTH TO SOUTH. In 1935, friars traveled from New York and the Northeast to North Carolina to begin a long ministry at St. Anthony of Padua Parish in Asheville. Friars still serve in North Carolina, South Carolina, Georgia, and Florida. (HNPA.)

ST. FRANCIS, THIRTY-FIRST STREET. Here is the early interior of St. Francis Church, which was a "service church" before anyone knew what that meant, in Midtown Manhattan. In 1904, the parish began to offer a "printers' Mass" at 2:30 a.m. on Sundays for newspaper printers ending their shift. The parish was the first in the country to offer 12:15 p.m. daily Mass for office workers on their lunch hour. (HNPA.)

ST. FRANCIS, SERVICE CHURCH. St. Francis parish was founded to serve German-speaking immigrants, but over the years, it opened its doors to all. In 1930, during the Great Depression, Br. Gabriel Mehler, the porter of the parish and friary, began what became known as the Breadline to serve the hungry. The Breadline still feeds hungry people every day. (HNPA.)

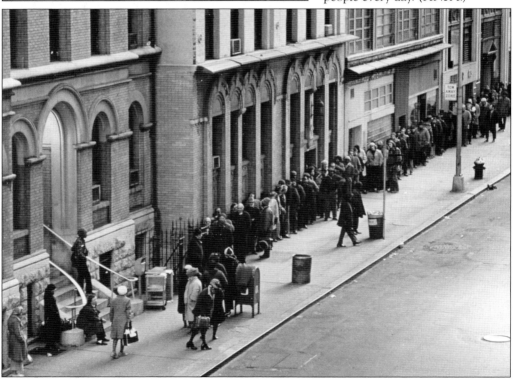

TO BOSTON, MASSACHUSETTS. The friars desired to establish themselves in Boston as well as New York, and in 1927, they were able to do so when Cardinal William Henry O'Connell, something of a wheeler-dealer, said that he would welcome them if they bought his former home in Brookline. So with the purchase of the house, the friars opened St. Francis Retreat House. (HNPA.)

EVOLVING PARISHES AND MINISTRIES. Founded by immigrants, the ministries of the friars continue to address the needs of new generations of immigrants, as seen here in a procession for Our Lady of Guadalupe's feast day, which begins in Butler, New Jersey, and concludes with a bilingual Mass in Pompton Lakes. (HNPA.)

MISSIONS TO CHINA. By 1948, when this photograph of friars on their annual retreat at the Shashi Mission in China was taken, the friars of Holy Name province had already been in China for over 35 years. They survived Japanese occupation, but the Communist Chinese would force them out by 1952. (HNPA.)

MISSIONS IN JAPAN. Friars of Holy Name province arrived in Japan in 1949. Since 1957, the Franciscan Chapel Center in Tokyo has provided religious services and opportunities for fellowship to English-speaking Catholics from all around the world, as well as from Japan. (HNPA.)

MISSION FRIARS IN HABITS. This 1968 photograph shows a number of friars from Holy Name province serving as missionaries in Bolivia gathered together to visit with their minister provincial during one of his regular trips to the country to see how they were doing. (HNPA.)

MISSION FRIARS NOT IN HABITS. The zeal and ability of a number of friars in the 1960s and 1970s was recognized by the church as they were named missionary bishops, as seen here in the early 1970s. Pictured from left to right, Thomas Manning, Eustace Smith, Juan Landazuri Rickets, James Schuck, and Benedict Coscia served in Bolivia, Lebanon, Peru, and Brazil. (HNPA.)

CAJETAN BAUMANN, ARCHITECT. The friars were invited to staff Holy Cross Church in the Bronx in 1921. The modern Holy Cross Church, built in 1968 and pictured here, was designed by Br. Cajetan Baumann, a Franciscan friar and noted architect. It is one of many churches and religious houses that he designed. For over 30 years, Holy Cross served as a home for postulants for the province. (HNPA.)

MYCHAL JUDGE AND FIRE CHAPLAINS. The friars of the province have a strong tradition of ministry with firefighters in both the United States and Lima, Peru. Here, John O'Connor (left) and Chris Keenan, two firefighter chaplains, remember Mychal Judge, who was killed in the line of duty on 9/11. (HNPA.)

DOMINIC TERNAN. A participant in the invasion of Normandy, Dominic Ternan was killed by sniper fire less than two weeks later on June 19, 1944, near Valognes, France. He was the first of several American Franciscan friars to die on a World War II battlefield and was awarded a Silver Star. (HNPA.)

JUSTIN MCCARTHY. With a wry insight into Franciscan life and human nature, Justin McCarthy created the lovable cartoon character "Brother Juniper," who can be seen in the background of this photograph. The cartoon appeared in 185 newspapers in North and South America, as well as Italy and Spain, from 1958 to 1989. (HNPA.)

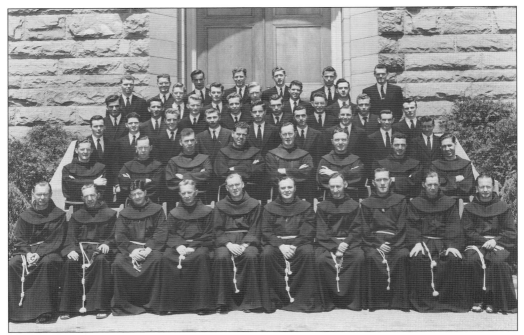

GOOD OLD DAYS. No doubt some of the incidents portrayed in the famous Brother Juniper cartoon had their origins in the antics of large groups of young friars and their teachers, such as these from about 1940, at St. Joseph Seraphic Seminary in Callicoon, New York. (HNPA.)

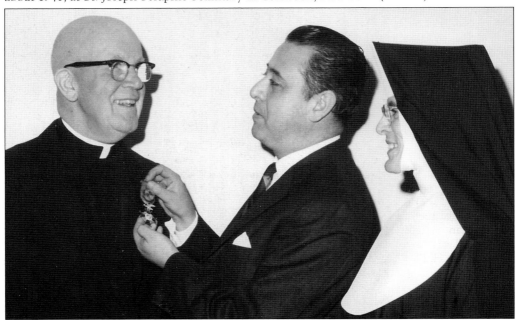

SISTERS AND BROTHERS. Since the time of Pamfilo da Magliano, the friars and the Franciscan Sisters of Allegany have worked together in the United States, Bolivia, Brazil, and Jamaica. Here, Mother Mary Jane Wheeler, head of the sisters, watches her brother Celsius Wheeler, at the time minister provincial, get pinned with an award in the late 1950s. (HNPA.)

AND THE FUN THEY HAD. In the days before the Internet, television, and even radio, there were friars who still sought to entertain one another and have a good time. In this undated photograph, it looks as if the drummers are the old-time friars who are going to keep a lively rhythm for the youngsters. (HNPA.)

THE STORIES THEY SHARED. Communication with laity and benefactors has always been important for sharing what Franciscans do. The *Friar*, a "magazine of Christian optimism," was published by Holy Name province from 1954 to 1979 to share the good news, popular catechesis, and apologetics, all in a lighthearted way. (HNPA.)

ST. ANTHONY SHRINE, BOSTON. Many ministries of the Franciscans of Holy Name province offer some sort of food assistance to those in need, either through parishes or service churches, such as St. Anthony Shrine in Boston. Here, Brian Cullinane and other friars are serving at the Shrine's food pantry. (HNPA.)

ST. FRANCIS INN, PHILADELPHIA. From humble beginnings in 1978 as a thrift shop, St. Francis Inn grew with the addition of meal service in 1979. The inn continues providing services with the help of volunteers, religious sisters, laypeople, and friars. (HNPA.)

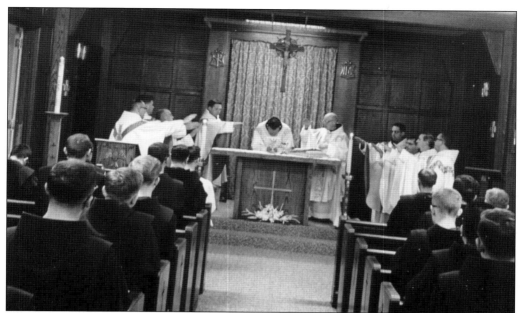

ONCE UPON A TIME. In the 1950s and through the 1960s, the celebration of the Eucharist, pictured at St. Francis Friary in Rye Beach, New Hampshire, was thought the gold standard of service and ministry to which young men would be drawn. Times changes, and the facility became a retreat house from 1967 until closing in 1994. (HNPA.)

love ...

lived in service

FRANCISCAN VOLUNTEER MINISTRY

WWW.FRANCISCANVOLUNTEERMINISTRY.ORG

A ministry of the Franciscan Friars of Holy Name Province

A DIFFERENT CALL. With the shift away from the lifetime commitment to religious life once thought to be the norm for those seeking to serve others as inspired by Christ and St. Francis, the friars adopted ways to welcome others who sought to serve for a shorter period of time with the introduction of Franciscan Volunteer Ministry in 1989. (HNPA.)

BUT PROCLAMATION CONTINUES. The friars have been itinerant preachers of the Gospel since the time of Francis of Assisi himself, and that tradition has continued in Holy Name Province with a Mission Band founded in 1901 in Denver, which moved later to the Bronx and Paterson, New Jersey, and now continues as the Ministry of the Word. (HNPA.)

TO ALL THE WORLD. In 1951, as the mission fields of China were closed to Western missionaries by the Chinese Communist government, the friars opened a language school for new missionaries who began to arrive in Japan from the United States and from other Franciscan communities from around the world. (HNPA.)

Four

ST. BARBARA PROVINCE

St. Barbara Province is named for Mission Santa Barbara, the historical link between the two Franciscan eras in the United States. Mission Santa Barbara was founded in 1786, and Franciscan friars have been in Santa Barbara ever since, through many ups and downs. From 1786 until 1821, California was part of the Spanish Empire. The friars administered not only the mission churches, which exist today, but also vast tracts of land in the name of the Spanish Crown. By government policy, on this land, once-nomadic Native Americans were gathered with the intention of forming them into Spanish citizens. After independence in 1821, the Mexican government claimed everything once held by the royal government, and secularized the missions, replacing Franciscans with lay administrators.

With secularization, vast tracts of land were sold, Native Americans moved away, and mission buildings fell into ruin. But the Franciscans remained in Santa Barbara. By 1885, the friars left in Santa Barbara were incorporated into Sacred Heart Province. Some St. Louis friars came West and also went to work among German-speaking immigrants. Other friars established missions among Native Americans in Arizona. Vocations from the West were encouraged with schools to form friars, and the Province of St. Barbara was established in 1915. Later, the friars added retreat ministry and social service ministry among the poor to their core ministries of parishes and schools, feeding the spirit and the bodies of many people who came to them.

Dn. Rl del Illmo Sor. Dr. D. Franco Garcia Diego primer Obispo
hijo del Apostolico Colegio de Na Sra de Guadalupe de Zacatecas

FRANCISCO DIEGO GARCIA Y MORENO. Born in 1785 in the Mexican state of Jalisco, Francisco Diego Garcia y Moreno entered the Franciscans at the Apostolic College of Guadalupe and was ordained a priest in 1808. Apostolic colleges were a home base, in this case in Zacatecas, for the training of missionary friars and then sending them off to work in particular mission areas. After fulfilling a number of other responsibilities, the future bishop went to California as head of the missions in 1832, and in 1839, the Mexican government suggested to the pope that he be named the first bishop of both Upper (Alta) and Lower (Baja) California. He was ordained bishop in 1840 and arrived in San Diego in 1841, which was supposed to be his see, or headquarters city, but he went on to Santa Barbara in 1842, where he remained until his death in 1846. Because their friar bishop was in Santa Barbara, the remaining friars in California gathered around him, making Santa Barbara, and not San Diego, the point of continuity between the old and the new. (SBPA.)

PADRES DECADES APART. Above, eight Franciscan friars, five of Irish descent and three originally from Mexico, posed for a formal photograph of the community at Mission Santa Barbara about 1883. They were the remnant of the friars who had once staffed 21 missions in California. Those of Irish descent had joined the Franciscans after arriving in California as individual immigrants. Those of Mexican origin predated US annexation in 1846. Fourth from the right, with lots of knots on his cord, Francisco Sanchez inspired the fictional friar, ironically described as "ascetically thin," in the 1884 best-selling novel *Ramona.* Below, another group of friars posed at Mission Santa Barbara in 1965. They were the "Padre Choirsters," a group of Franciscan theology students who performed music from the colonial era at the annual Santa Barbara Fiesta. (SBPA.)

FROM ROME TO CALIFORNIA. The mission at Santa Barbara has been rebuilt a number of times, but by the time that the friars from St. Louis arrived in 1885, it looked as shown in this photograph from about 1925. The facade of the mission church is based on the work of the Roman architect Vitruvius, and there are similar edifices among colonial Franciscan missions in Central Mexico. (SBPA.)

THE NEED TO REBUILD. Mission San Luis Rey in Oceanside, California, was founded in 1798, but by the time that the Franciscan friars returned in 1892, it was in severe need of rebuilding, as seen in this photograph from about that time. Reconstruction began in 1895. Besides being a center for the local Catholic community, for many decades friar students studied philosophy here. (SBPA.)

SPANISH AND GERMAN. One of the first places that the newly arrived German-speaking friars went to work to serve immigrants from Germany was Oakland, California, where St. Elizabeth Parish was established in 1892. But the architecture for the church building was kept in keeping with the Spanish/Mexican heritage of California. (SBPA.)

ST. MARY IN PHOENIX. The parish of St. Mary was founded in Phoenix in the territory of Arizona in 1892, and the Franciscans took responsibility for the church in 1895. Twenty years later, as this 1915 photograph shows, what would become St. Mary Basilica, where Pope St. John Paul II prayed in 1987, had become a beautiful local landmark. (SBPA.)

A NEW PROVINCE. St. Barbara Province held its first provincial chapter in Santa Barbara in January 1916. In this photograph of most of the friars of the new province, taken in the sacred garden courtyard of Mission Santa Barbara at that time, it appears that the farther back you go in the picture the younger the friars! (SBPA.)

NEW PROVINCIAL LEADERSHIP. The newly installed provincial administration of St. Barbara Province at the 1916 provincial chapter included Hugolinus Storff, the one with the beard seated in the front center. Like the rest of the initial new province leadership, he had German roots and had grown up as a friar in Sacred Heart Province. (SBPA.)

EDUCATING YOUNG FRIARS. Classes for young men seeking to become Franciscans began soon after the Sacred Heart Province friars arrived to help at Mission Santa Barbara. These 11 very young men posed for a formal portrait with their friar instructors as they began classes in 1896. (SBPA.)

PLAY BALL! By 1917, when this photograph was taken, St. Anthony High School Seminary was a going concern and thoroughly with-it in every way, as evidenced by this photograph of the baseball team with its friar coach. (SBPA.)

HIGHER STUDIES. From the 1890s until the 1970s, St. Barbara Province, like many religious communities of men throughout the United States, organized and usually provided an in-house course of education that ran from precollege, through college philosophy courses, and finally, graduate studies in theology in preparation for ordination, with a spiritual year of the novitiate for both priesthood and lay brother candidates. These are the novices of 1965–1966. (SBPA.)

TIME OFF FROM STUDIES. In the 1920s, these student friars, who are nearing the completion of their preparation for ordination to the priesthood, took some time off for relaxation. The photograph was taken somewhere in the foothills just to the north of Santa Barbara. (SBPA.)

Earthquake! On June 29, 1925, Santa Barbara suffered a magnitude 6.8 earthquake, which damaged the entire community, including mission and seminary. Pictured on the left with the beard, Zephyrin Engelhardt, one of the seminary professors and a noted authority on California colonial mission history, looks over damage to the base of one of the mission church's towers. (SBPA.)

Studies Interrupted. With the damage caused by the 1925 earthquake preventing use of the of the mission and the seminary, the friars lived in tents and conducted all religious services outside for two months. (SBPA.)

SCHOOLS REQUIRE SCHOLARS. Owen Da Silva composed, performed, and made music a vital part of the life of St. Barbara Province friars from 1925 to 1967. He also founded retreat houses from California to New Mexico. Here, he is seen in the choir loft in Mission Santa Barbara with an intercom phone nearby to allow communication with the church sacristy. (SBPA.)

MAYNARD GEIGER. A noted historian of the California missions, Maynard wrote extensively on the life of the first president of the California missions, Junipero Serra. He organized the mission archive library in Santa Barbara and, in so doing, laid the groundwork for a great number of scholars who would come after him. (SBPA.)

CHRISTIAN MONDOR. After teaching and making music fun for over 20 years in Oregon, where he founded Serra High School in Salem, Christian Mondor (pictured second from left, playing banjo) moved south and spent decades surfing off the coast of Huntington Beach, California. There he is credited with starting an annual Blessing of the Waves. (SBPA.)

VIRGIL CORDANO. A part of Santa Barbara from 1934 until he died in 2008, Virgil Cordano taught many friar students and thousands of lay learners. A professorship in Catholic studies was named and endowed in his honor at the University of California at Santa Barbara. Here, he is taking part in the annual Santa Barbara Old Spanish Days Fiesta. (SBPA.)

NATIVE AMERICAN MISSIONS AGAIN. The Franciscan efforts that led to St. Barbara Province began with 18th-century attempts to proclaim the Gospel to Native Americans. In the 20th century, those efforts were concentrated in Arizona and New Mexico. Bonaventure Oblasser, shown here at a mission church, worked among the Tohono O'odham, or "People of the Desert," in Southern Arizona for over 30 years. (SBPA.)

LAMBERT FREMDLING. Escaping Nazi Germany in 1940, Lambert Fremdling came to the United States to be ordained and began 40 years of ministry among the Tohono O'odham, leading him to become an expert in their language and to receive the singular honor of being buried among the people as one of them. Here, he is with Tohono O'odham friends in 1967. (SBPA.)

FIDELIS MILLER. Transportation of Native American students across vast stretches of reservation land to get them to school required careful attention to buses. Here, Br. Fidelis Miller keeps the St. Johns Indian School bus in good repair in Komatke, Arizona, in 1965. (SBPA.)

TELLING THE MISSION STORY. The *Way* magazine began publication in 1950, in part as a means of raising money to help support the friars and the missions both spiritually and financially. Here, Br. Brendan Mitchell (standing) and Fr. Francis X. Maynard work on the publication in the 1960s. (SBPA.)

PROPHET OF MERCY. Seen here in a photograph from 1956, Alfred Boeddeker had responded to a need six years earlier and opened St. Anthony Dining Room in the Tenderloin neighborhood of San Francisco, which has grown into the St. Anthony Foundation, a multifaceted social service agency serving hundreds of thousands of people annually in dozens of different ways. The dining room has served over 42 million meals. (SBPA.)

HUGH NOONAN. Shown here with his lay Franciscan cofounders, Helen Payne (center) and Juanita Vaughn (right), Hugh Noonan (left) founded the St. Francis Center in Los Angeles in 1972 to bring relief to the homeless and poor who lacked food. In 1946, he had created the *Hour of St. Francis* for radio, which eventually ran on over 500 radio stations nationwide. (SBPA.)

LOUIS VITALE. Founding the Nevada Desert Experience to bring people to pray at the Nevada test site of nuclear weapons, Louis Vitale never feared to "cross the line" in peaceful protest of unjust or immoral government actions. A true follower of St. Francis, Louis Vitale often prayed for, and with, the same law enforcement officers who arrested him hundreds of times. (SBPA.)

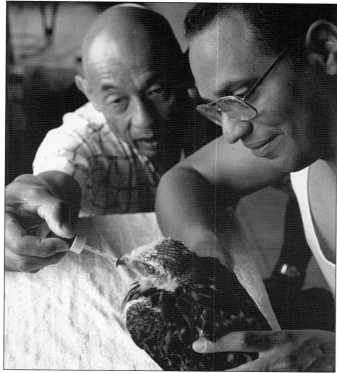

EMERY TANG. Known for gentle and provocative preaching, writing, and photography, Emery Tang liked to point out the "sacred ordinary" that others often missed. Here, shown on the left, he is helping nurse an injured bird in Guymas, Mexico. (SBPA.)

RETREAT MINISTRY. Between 1942 and 2007, the Franciscans of St. Barbara Province engaged in lots of retreat ministry, building a total of nine retreat centers, including the Casa Paz y Bien (House of Peace and Good) in Scottsdale, Arizona. Here, in a publicity photograph, a friar greets a young married couple coming for a weekend retreat in the 1950s. (SBPA.)

CASA PAZ Y BIEN. The Casa Paz y Bien was built on the far outskirts of Phoenix, then a city of half a million people. But the empty space all around this outdoor altar of Our Lady of Guadalupe at the edge of the retreat house complex, as it was dedicated in 1951, would soon be filled with homes just beyond the edge of an enlarged retreat center. (SBPA.)

A RESTFUL RETREAT. In the midst of growing cities and urban sprawl, Franciscans offered a place of peace and quiet in beautiful settings to those who came to pray and to simply get away from the busy activities of their lives, as seen here at San Damiano Retreat, built in 1961 in Danville, California. (SBPA.)

A PRAYERFUL RETREAT. Retreats also served as the means for people seeking to join with others in prayer and make a closer connection to God. In the 1960s, retreats in the tradition of the charismatic renewal often featured prayer circles and spontaneous prayer, as pictured here in the chapel at St. Francis Retreat in San Juan Bautista, California. (SBPA.)

HISTORIANS AND HISTORY. Joseph Chinnici won awards for both his teaching and writing of history, but in the 1990s, he made history. Serving as minister provincial of the St. Barbara Province when the province and the entire Roman Catholic Church began to deal with sexual abuse scandals, he responded with farsightedness and pastoral programs to heal the abuse that had happened and prevent future abuse. (SBPA.)

ARCHIVISTS AND HISTORY. Br. Timothy Arthur was given a room full of boxes containing papers, photographs, and artifacts and turned them into the archives of St. Barbara Province. But he also helped history along, giving his friend Cesar Chavez a quiet place for retreat and renewal at Mission San Miguel many times during the 1960s as Chavez struggled for farmworkers and civil rights for Chicanos. (SBPA.)

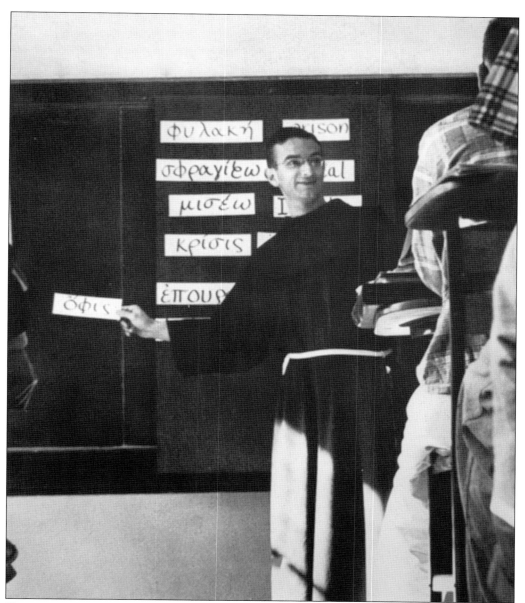

Teachers and History. John Vaughn was born in 1928 and professed Franciscan vows in 1948. He was ordained in 1955. After time in parish work, he was sent off for studies of Spanish in Mexico, and after teaching at the high school level, he was sent to Rome for higher studies. In 1969, he became novice master, pastor, and guardian in Sacramento, California, all at the same time. He was elected vicar provincial in 1973 and minister provincial in 1976, but only served until 1979, when he was elected minister general of the worldwide Order of Friars Minor. For 12 years, he oversaw new mission efforts of the order into Africa and the countries of the former Soviet Union, while stressing the formation of smaller, more localized provinces of friars in place of large provinces with large distant mission territories. After completing two terms as minister general, he returned to being novice director and then worked on the cause of the canonization of Junipero Serra before dying in 2016. (SBPA.)

PASSING ON THE ANCIENT TRADITION.
Kenan Osborne, here with a student,
taught generations of students on the
graduate school level all around the
world, offering them keen Franciscan
insights into the great questions
about God, human beings, and their
relationships to each other in his
lectures, in his writings, and in the
joyful way that he lived his life. (SBPA.)

PASSING ON THE MODERN TRADITION.
Br. Maurice "Mo" Peltier was porter at
Mission San Luis Rey in Oceanside,
California. Fourth graders in
California study and make field trips
to Franciscan missions. Brother Mo
became part of that experience for
thousands of visitors. He connected
them to missionaries and Native
Americans of long ago, while offering
a little advice about how to live well
with others in the future. (SBPA.)

Five

ASSUMPTION OF THE BLESSED VIRGIN MARY PROVINCE

The Province of the Assumption of the Blessed Virgin Mary began with a desire to serve immigrants, but in this case, it was not the desire of a bishop, but instead the desire of Augustine Zeytz, a Franciscan lay brother, to serve his fellow Poles. He knew that in a strange land, keeping alive their faith and traditions would provide the strength to endure many hardships.

Augustine Zeytz saw need for Franciscan ministry among Polish immigrants in Pennsylvania, where, in 1873, he ministered alone as best he could. He returned to Europe, and by 1888, he persuaded others to join him in Pulaski, Wisconsin. Lay leadership became part of the community's way of doing things. Progress did not come easily. In 1894, the friars in Wisconsin were placed under Sacred Heart Province in the midst of much community strife. After matters stabilized, a step was taken toward independence. A commissariat was established in 1910. In 1939, the Province of the Assumption of the Blessed Virgin Mary came into being. In 1947, Byzantine Franciscan friars began ministry in the United States as St. Mary of the Angels Custody, and in 1998, they were joined to the Assumption Province.

From the beginning, the friars have lived out a bold dedication to justice, placing a great emphasis on the role of lay brothers, and a dedication to equality in society, stressing action where it was needed for the advancement of civil rights and social justice.

Brother Augustine Zeytz, Founder of Assumption Commissariat, Pulaski, Wis.

FOUNDING FRIAR, AUGUSTINE ZEYTZ. Fleeing anti–Roman Catholic Russian rule in occupied Poland in 1872, Augustine traveled to America and spent time with friars of both the Immaculate Conception and St. John the Baptist Custodies, before finding fellow Polish immigrants in the mining towns of Pennsylvania. He entered into the lives of the immigrants and ministered to them, working in the mines, putting his medical training to use, and evangelizing them in their native language. He became convinced of the need for Polish Franciscan friars in the United States. He returned to Europe in 1881 to persuade others to join him. His efforts went slowly. In 1886, he returned to America, still alone, but with the promise of land for a friary in Wisconsin. In 1888, three friars finally joined Augustine. But all did not go well. The community grew slowly, and tension mounted between the lay brothers and the priests. By 1896, ten lay brothers, including Augustine Zeytz, transferred to Sacred Heart Province from the Wisconsin foundation. He died September 3, 1914, still somewhat a friar in exile. (SHPA.)

"If You Build It . . ." Receiving a gift of land in Pulaski, Wisconsin, from land developer John Hoff, who thought that the presence of Polish Franciscan friars would entice other Polish immigrants to the area, Assumption of the Blessed Virgin Mary began as a small church with the lay friars left to tend things in Pulaski while the ordained friars made a large circuit of Polish communities in the area to provide sacramental ministry and raise money. (ABVMPA.)

"They Will Come." Immigrants did arrive in the Pulaski area, and the community grew, with a great devotion to their Roman Catholic faith and a great pride in their church, as shown in these photographs of a celebration not long after the turn of the 20th century. By 1910, a total of 35 friars, of whom 15 were clerics and 20 were lay brothers, lived at Assumption Friary. (ABVMPA.)

CELEBRATING GROWTH. Special celebrations of their Catholic faith became big and important community events at Assumption Parish in Pulaski, as seen here in a photograph of the Corpus Christi procession gathered in 1953 outside Assumption Church, which, due to the hard work of the people, was judged the largest Catholic church in rural America. (ABVMPA.)

REACHING THE ZENITH. By 1965, Assumption Parish in Pulaski was a huge operation in close cooperation with Assumption Province. The complex contained the parish church and school, friary, sisters' convent, farm, cemetery, and a trade school open to friar students and others, as well as a professional print shop, which produced hundreds of thousands of copies of Franciscan publications in Polish and English. (ABVMPA.)

EDUCATION FOR ALL. In 1954, St. Joseph School, which served both aspiring lay brother Franciscans and other local students (note the plaid shirts in the second row), was dedicated as a place for learning all sorts of industrial arts and trades. (ABVMPA.)

WITH A HIGHER PURPOSE. Education at St. Joseph School was intended not only to teach practical skills but also to instill a lifelong devotion to the Catholic faith, as witnessed by young men professing their vows as tertiary Franciscans, devoted to Franciscan ideals, but not necessarily becoming a friar. Though these newly initiated tertiary brothers were probably all at least considering religious life in 1954. (ABVMPA.)

To Work with My Hands. Francis of Assisi encouraged his brothers from the very beginning to work with their hands to avoid idleness, the enemy of the soul. Here, only slightly older friars at St. Joseph School are passing on tailoring skills to their younger brothers. (ABVMPA.)

Training for Usefulness. Lay brothers played important roles in keeping things running smoothly in all sorts of Franciscan missions, from isolated foreign and rural areas to busy urban centers. A variety of skills were often needed by the same friar, and at St. Joseph School, many skills were shared among the brothers including the repair of small electrical appliances, pictured here. (ABVMPA.)

Following the Plans. With one young tertiary brother making a presentation to his peers under the watchful eye of an older friar, the importance of knowing the materials with which woodworking was done, as well as how to follow plans, was inculcated among the brothers who would go on to build and repair many things. (ABVMPA.)

The Fruits of One's Labor. With dozens of young students to be fed, the friary farm in Pulaski was an important part of the overall operation of the religious community. Here, Brothers Bruce and Dennis are washing up mechanical milking machines in the late 1950s, maybe even dreaming of ice cream. (ABVMPA.)

PULLING TOGETHER HANDS AND HEARTS. In the early 1950s, Br. Tom Kaminski is hard at work keeping in good repair the engine for the St. Francis School bus in Greenwood, Mississippi. The bus and school were important parts of the efforts that the friars made in west-central Mississippi to overcome poverty and prejudice. Frs. Nathaniel Machesky and Bonaventure Bolda led these efforts with Franciscan religious sisters and the Pax Christi Institute, a pious diocesan union of laypeople. In 1954, the state legislature of Mississippi seriously proposed closing all the public schools in the state if racial integration were forced upon them by the federal government. Beyond St. Francis School, dedicated in 1953, the friars used "Catholic information centers" to reach out to local people who knew almost nothing of the Catholic Church. The Catholic information centers provided social services and a means for the people to see Catholic faith at work. They served to evangelize by attraction, a Franciscan tradition. (ABVMPA.)

NATHANIEL MACHESKY. Nathaniel Machesky, though only one of several of his brothers involved in the civil rights movement, became the one friar of Assumption Province most identified with the Mississippi missions from their founding right on through the 1960s fight for racial integration, as well as through the violent backlash to that struggle. (ABVMPA.)

ADRIAN KOLANCZYK.
Brother Adrian
not only provided
gardening and
masonry skills for
the benefit of the
Mississippi missions,
but he was also an
organist and choir
director, as illustrated
here with a Christmas
morning children's
concert of carols in
1954. (ABVMPA.)

SERGIUS WROBLEWSKI. Of the young friars who came of age as Franciscans during the era of struggles for civil rights in the South, none would become more dedicated to issues of peace and justice than Sergius Wroblewski. Here, he is seen proclaiming the theme of that movement, "We Shall Overcome," on his placard while leading a civil rights protest at Christ the King Seminary in West Chicago, Illinois. (ABVMPA.)

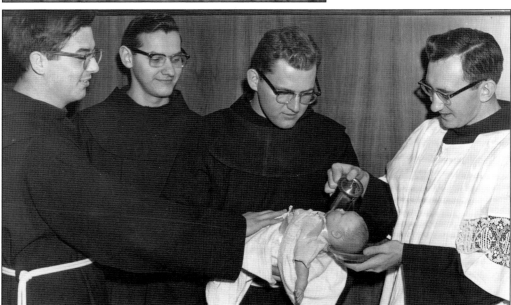

WILLIE GULAS. William Gulas, here practicing the baptism of an infant while in studies at Christ the King Seminary, would go on to ordination and a storied Franciscan life, which included service to his brothers as minister provincial, before his death as the result of a tragic act of violence in 2002. (ABVMPA.)

LAST STOP BEFORE ORDINATION. Christ the King Seminary was built in West Chicago in the mid-1950s, during a time of unprecedented growth among all Roman Catholic religious communities and of the whole Catholic population in the United States. With changing times and fewer vocations after the heyday of the 1950s, Christ the King was closed in 1970, eventually sold, and torn down. (ABVMPA.)

MODERN DESIGN.
The design of the
chapel at Christ
the King Seminary
boldly embraced
the latest and
most modern
design elements
of the 1950s, with
three-quarters
round seating
and the blondest
wood possible for
the furnishings.
(ABVMPA.)

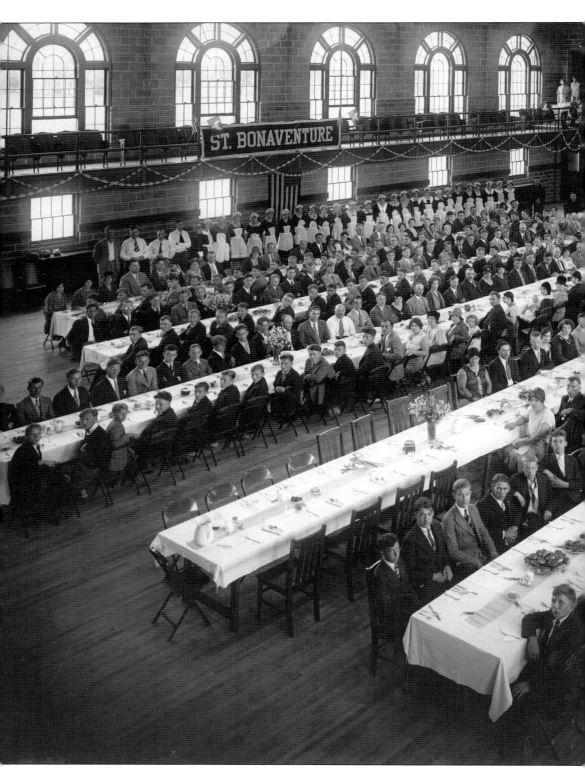

St. Bonaventure–Sturtevant.
Just at the time that the first
foundations of the Assumption of
the Blessed Virgin Mary Province
were laid in the 1880s, the
practice of establishing minor or
preparatory seminaries also took
off throughout the Franciscan
Order around the world. The
idea at the time was to provide
a setting that would prevent
young men from becoming
too worldly. In addition, in the
United States, minor seminaries
provided the means for Catholic
sons of immigrants to get a good,
solid, and Catholic-oriented
education, when other schools
were largely unavailable to
them. The minor seminary of
Assumption Province was first
located in Pulaski, but in 1922,
it moved to Sturtevant, then
called Corliss, Wisconsin, where
it remained until closing in
1983. In 1930, the friars went
all out to dedicate the school's
new gymnasium. (ABVMPA.)

ORCHESTRA
1939-40

WELL-ROUNDED YOUNG SCHOLARS. The high school seminary experience was intended to provide the background to allow young men to explore many different means of giving glory to God through music, art, and literature. The Gospel of Jesus was the good news, and they wanted to proclaim it in every way possible. (ABVMPA.)

TRAGEDY STRIKES. A fire caused by faulty wiring led to the destruction of the seminary dormitory and faculty housing in 1956. All 169 students were safe, but their personal property and the dissertation work of Roderick Drag, one of their professors, was all lost. Here, Arthur Jankowski, the rector, looks to the future of the school after the fire. (ABVMPA.)

EAGER STUDENTS. Returned to full operation by 1960, St. Bonaventure continued to be the first point of entry for many young men with aspirations to become Franciscans friars, as seen in this photograph, undoubtedly intended for publicity purposes. (ABVMPA.)

NEXT STOP, NOVITIATE. After high school graduation, the next formal step of Franciscan formation was the novitiate, which involved a radical turning away from the vanities of the world. This 1951 photograph of novices with hair slowly returning to shaved heads shows one way "the world" was set aside. (ABVMPA.)

LAKE GENEVA NOVITIATE. For years, Assumption Province conducted the novitiate at Lake Geneva, where the original building was a mansion with elegant appointments donated to the friars, which is visible in this 1953 photograph of the novices. In these elegant surroundings, the novices were actually preparing for very different surroundings, as the friars had recently begun ministry among poor African Americans in Mississippi and in the far-flung islands of the Philippines. (ABVMPA.)

VOLLEYBALL IN THE NOVITIATE. This 1962 photograph of the novitiate shows that it is possible to exercise and have fun at the same time, even in a Franciscan habit and sandals. These novices were joining a province at its peak with 435 professed members, including 167 lay brothers. (ABVMPA.)

IMPORTANT SANDALS. Br. David Typek, shown in his cobbler shop in Pulaski, produced sandals for generations of Franciscan novices and friars. Brother David must have made very good sandals and in other ways earned the respect and admiration of his peers, as he was repeatedly elected a delegate to the provincial chapter, the highest governing body of the province. (ABVMPA.)

PROUD NEW FOOTWEAR. These novices showing off their new sandals in 1962 could well be wearing some of Br. David Typek's handiwork. (ABVMPA.)

ON TO PHILOSOPHY. For a number of years, after the novitiate, young friars who were going to be ordained priests studied philosophy in Burlington, Wisconsin. Here, a group is singing in a procession during a ceremony that illustrated the connection between the people and the friars. (ABVMPA.)

FRIARS AND PEOPLE. Here, in 1962, the friar philosophy students and their faculty gather on the steps of the chapel at Burlington during an annual celebration, which included a lot of laypeople from the community. (ABVMPA.)

A Place for Healing. St. Mary of the Angels and the Portiuncula Chapel dedicated to her in Assisi have long been associated with healing and reconciliation, so friars have often built replicas of the chapel, which have become places for pilgrimage on their own, like this one in Burlington. (ABVMPA.)

Healing in Different Times. Though later thought strange, in 1960, not many people at the time would have given a second thought to cigarette-smoking participants in a procession for healing. Here, young friars in Burlington help wheel them along. (ABVMPA.)

A Missionary Send-Off. In 1966, Br. Gus Fraszczak, the tall one shaking hands with his minister provincial, Dacian Blume, headed off to the Philippines, where he joined many other friar missionaries of the province. Still in the Philippines, Brother Gus has provided medical care for tens of thousands of Filipinos and friars. (ABVMPA.)

Contemporary Music. Just as the electric guitar was coming into vogue, Br. Kevin Schroeder, in the front, second from the left, and a number of other young friars formed "the Cords." Thus, Kevin began a career in media, continuing the long involvement of Assumption Province in print and other forms of mass communication, all to give praise to God and proclaim the Gospel. (ABVMPA.)

Six

OUR LADY OF GUADALUPE PROVINCE

Our Lady of Guadalupe Province, coming into being in 1985, took up a Franciscan heritage tracing back to the 16th and 17th centuries. Franciscan missionaries from Spain, and later Mexico, remained with the people of the Southwest, both Native Americans and Hispanic settlers from then until the mid-19th century. About 50 years later, in 1897, Katharine Drexel, SBS, had begun to found Catholic schools and grew concerned that the Navajo reservation had no Catholic missionaries. But to found a school to be staffed by her religious community of sisters on the reservation, she was adamant that there also be male religious priests and brothers to help. She appealed to the Franciscan friars of St. John the Baptist Province in Cincinnati, who agreed to send missionaries.

Three friars arrived at St. Michaels, Arizona, on the Navajo reservation in October 1898. They found it a desolate place, but through a cold winter, they worked at learning the Navajo language and something of the Navajo culture. Within 20 years, they had branched out to renew the presence of Franciscans among Native Americans and Hispanics nearly to the Grand Canyon in the west, to Santa Fe to the northeast, and to Roswell and Carlsbad in the southeast. Eventually, the number of friars from Cincinnati peaked at 100. The Province of Our Lady of Guadalupe was established in 1985, the youngest of Franciscan entities in the United States, but among ancient peoples who had first heard of Franciscans 400 years earlier.

FOUNDING SISTER, KATHARINE DREXEL. *A Philadelphia debutante, Katharine Drexel turned to helping African Americans and Native Americans at her parents' early deaths. At the suggestion of Pope Leo XIII, she founded the Sisters of the Blessed Sacrament (SBS), specifically to educate and serve these peoples, who 20 years after the end of Reconstruction in the South and the Indian Wars in the West were largely forgotten. She dreamed of founding a school on the Navajo Reservation, the largest Native American reservation in the country. St. Michael Indian School came from her efforts, after she persuaded Franciscan friars from Cincinnati to help. The work of those friars included persuading Navajo elders to voluntarily send children to "the sisters' school," at a time when the US government was forcing Native children to attend government-run schools. When the Navajo students first arrived at the school, their families would camp out nearby for weeks to see how the sisters were really treating their children. At 96 years old and still a spiritual force when she died in 1955, St. Katharine Drexel was canonized in 2000. (OLGPA.)*

Placidus Buerger. To get the mission started on the Navajo Reservation, Katharine Drexel purchased land with an old trading post on it at a place she insisted be named St. Michaels, after her childhood home. The trading post became a very cozy mission chapel, friars' dormitory, and kitchen/sitting room, as the first three friar missionaries in 1898 suffered through a very cold winter. But that cold winter aided their evangelization efforts. The mission was miles from other dwellings but on a well-worn trail. Brother Placidus, pictured here in 1903, kept a fire in the kitchen stove, and the smoke rose straight up through the stovepipe into the cloudless winter sky and served as a beacon to cold travelers. The friars offered hospitality, began to learn Navajo words as visitors sipped the brothers' coffee, and made a reputation as good neighbors. (OLGPA.)

ANSELM WEBER. Born in Michigan in 1862, Anselm arrived with the first missionaries from Cincinnati in 1898 and remained in the Southwest until his death in 1921, serving as head of the mission from 1900. He was tireless in his efforts to evangelize the Navajo not only through religious instruction but also in practical day-to-day matters. He helped the Navajo organize their self-rule as a tribe, made numerous trips to Washington, DC, with delegations of the Navajo, and wrote countless words for many publications, all in an effort to secure the land and other resources that they so desperately needed. On at least three occasions, Anselm personally prevented the outbreak of violence between groups of Navajo and the US Army. His passionate desire for justice and what was right for the Navajo gave him an indomitable spirit, which allowed him to take on the federal government, while his own deep faith and spirituality served to let him do so in a way that led to reconciliation rather than conflict. (SJBPA.)

JUVENAL SCHNORBUS. The original leader of the three missionaries who came from Cincinnati to Arizona in 1898, Juvenal was a native of Cincinnati, Ohio, and 36 years old. He spent only a couple of years on the Navajo Reservation before returning to the Midwest. He came back to New Mexico and served briefly at Jemez Pueblo, Roswell, and Carlsbad. He was only 50 years old when he died in Cincinnati. (OLGPA.)

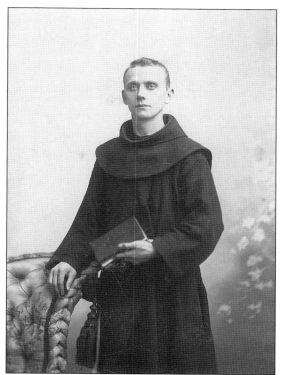

LEOPOLD OSTERMANN. Arriving in 1900 as half of the second wave of Cincinnati missionaries among the Navajo, Leopold Ostermann excelled in linguistics, teaching Latin, Greek, German, and French in the East before becoming fluent in Navajo. A writer, he contributed over 100 articles to the *St. Anthony Messenger* to help spread the news of the Navajo missions. (OLGPA.)

BERARD HAILE. Arriving with Leopold Ostermann in 1900, Berard Haile probably had no idea that he had begun an over 60-year-long adventure with the Navajo people, their culture, and their language. He once wrote, "Here we had a strange people. It seemed to me that one had to study their customs, their outlook on life, on the universe, natural phenomena, their concepts on the origin of man, vegetation and animals, before one could approach them on religious matters." He went to work producing the first method of writing the Navajo language and with the help of other friars was largely responsible for an ethnological dictionary of the Navajo language, which is still an important resource for scholars. His work was recognized and honored by several academic institutions and the Navajo tribe itself. And all along, his cigar was as important to him as his meticulous charts and notes, both pictured here. (OLGPA.)

PEÑA BLANCA, NEW MEXICO. In 1900, Archbishop Peter Bourgade invited friars from Cincinnati to Peña Blanca. By the time these friars gathered there for a retreat in 1938, Peña Blanca was a hub of Franciscan activity. Angelico Chavez (front row, left) and Pancratius Candelaria (front row, third from right) were significant friars in the Southwest for over half a century. Note the pocket watches visible under several friars' cowls. (OLGPA.)

ROSWELL, NEW MEXICO. In 1903, Mexican and American parishes were not integrated, so at the request of the archbishop of Santa Fe, St. John the Baptist "for the Spanish-speaking of Chaves County" and St. Peter for English speakers were established by the friars in Roswell. In this photograph from about 70 years later, American Knights of Columbus process at the St. John's parish homecoming. (OLGPA.)

ARCHBISHOP ALBERT DAEGER. "Padre Alberto," as he was known to his many Hispanic parishioners all over New Mexico, was a surprise choice to be the first non-Frenchman to head the Archdiocese of Santa Fe when named in 1919. His way of doing things, including ordaining local Hispanics, was not always welcomed by the mostly French local diocesan clergy. Pictured here with his brother Vigil Daeger, the archbishop died in a tragic accident in 1932, only 60 years old. (OLGPA.)

SANTA FE, NEW MEXICO. As archbishop, Albert Daeger decided to bring Franciscan friars to serve the city of Santa Fe for the first time in over a century. They staffed the cathedral of St. Francis and several surrounding missions, both Hispanic and Native American, for 80 years, returning the cathedral to diocesan administration in January 2000. Here, in the 1940s, from left to right, Patrick MacAuley, Jerome Hesse, and Barnabas Meyer celebrate in the chapel of Santa Fe's St. Vincent Hospital. (OLGPA.)

GALLUP, NEW MEXICO. The 1910 Franciscan assumption of ministry in this city at the edge of the Navajo Reservation was part of Anselm Weber's strategy of expansion. Ministry in Gallup took on a life of its own with many ethnic groups, resulting in the eventual formation of two Franciscan parishes, Sacred Heart and St. Francis, and the establishment of the Diocese of Gallup. In 1949, Bishop Espelage celebrates church growth with an outdoor rally. (OLGPA.)

BISHOP BERNARD ESPELAGE. In late 1939, the Diocese of Gallup was created from adjoining sections of the Archdiocese of Santa Fe and the Diocese of Tucson. In 1940, Bernard Espelage was named the first bishop of the new diocese. He worked tirelessly in building up the diocese and its clergy, as well as attending Vatican II, during his 29 years as bishop. (OLGPA.)

LAGUNA PUEBLO, NEW MEXICO. In 1699, people of several different Indian pueblos in New Mexico came together to form a new pueblo, the only one founded after the arrival of the Spanish. They asked the Franciscan friars serving New Mexico to send them ministers, and as proof of the sincerity of their request, they built their church before a friar arrived. Here, in the 1960s people, friars, a sister, and the bishop, wearing the hat with a pom behind the friar, prepare to celebrate a big event. (OLGPA.)

AGNELLUS LAMMERT. Dying unexpectedly in 1952 on the day of the celebration of his 25th anniversary of ordination, Agnellus was accorded the singular honor by the people of Laguna of being buried by St. Joseph Church. Like St. Francis, he had literally built churches and, in so doing, had helped people, such as the parishioners pictured with him here, build the church in their hearts. (OLGPA.)

John Evangelist Uhl. As the issue of whether to form Our Lady of Guadalupe Province was being debated, John Evangelist Uhl was a fierce proponent of a new province in the Southwest. He died only six months after the province was established, and thus received the title "Firstborn (into Heaven) of the Province." He was the second Franciscan friar to be given the honor of being buried by St. Joseph Church in Laguna Pueblo. (OLGPA.)

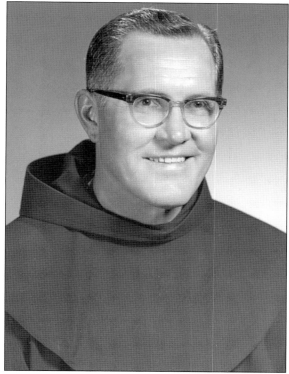

Kenneth Robertson. The third of the trio of Franciscan friars buried by St. Joseph Church in Laguna, Kenneth Robertson was not only a missionary there in the 1950s but also went on to be a widely admired pastor serving throughout the diocese of Gallup. He served as the rector of Sacred Heart Cathedral and then as pastor of Sacred Heart Parish in Farmington, where he built St. Mary Church and Parish. (OLGPA.)

THE PADRES HOUR. Cormac Antram was driving from one of his missions on the Navajo Reservation to another when he heard a Protestant preacher on the radio and asked himself the following question: "Why are there no Franciscans on the radio?" In May 1958, he began the *Padres' Hour*. He began recording the show with Helen and Lorenzo Yazzie. When age and ill health forced Cormac's retirement, Maynard Shurley, a Navajo friar took over the program. (OLGPA.)

REYNALDO RIVERA. In August 1982, Reynaldo, seen here in a relaxed moment, responded to a call "for a priest, any priest," to supply the last rites of the church to a dying man. The call was a ruse. Reynaldo's body was not found until days later after a massive search of the desert. His funeral was the largest ever seen in Santa Fe, and his murder remains unsolved. (OLGPA.)

DECISION MADE. The first and only time that the provincial chapter of St. John the Baptist Province met in the Southwest was at the College of Santa Fe in 1984. At that chapter, the friars voted to petition Minister General John Vaughn, here in the front center of the photograph, to form "a new entity" of friars in the Southwest. (SJBPA.)

JANUARY 3, 1985. In St. Francis Cathedral in Santa Fe, Minister General John Vaughn formally established the Province of Our Lady of Guadalupe in the midst of a church packed with bishops, friars, religious sisters, secular Franciscans, Hispanic New Mexicans, Pueblo and Navajo Indians, and well-wishers of every sort. Meldon Hickey, the first minister provincial, remembered the event in a formal letter soon afterwards. (OLGPA.)

THE FRANCISCANS
PROVINCE OF OUR LADY OF GUADALUPE

Post Office Box 12127
Albuquerque, New Mexico 87105

January 14, 1985

BROTHERS AND SISTERS:

Now that Our Lady of Guadalupe Province has been officially established by the decree of our Minister General, John Vaughn, we will have to begin to put into reality some of the visions, challenges and dreams that have gone into the planning.

That will, of course, take time, understanding, work, prayer and communication. However, all of the enthusiasm and support that was shown at the establishment, January 3, 1985, at St. Francis Cathedral, Santa Fe, will inspire us for many months and, hopefully, many years.

We of the newly formed Province of Our Lady of Guadalupe are very grateful for all of the support that has been given by the Province of St. John the Baptist in Cincinnati, and will maintain that close and fraternal friendship that has grown over the years.

We are also grateful for the men who still belong to the Province of St. John the Baptist, who, because of their love of the Southwest and the people of the Southwest, are willing to stay to work in the new Province, helping us to develop an even greater thrust of Franciscan charism in the Southwest.

We are also grateful to our Secular Franciscans; and we hope that they will become even more closely allied with us in spreading the vision of St. Francis of Assisi. With more people instilled with the Franciscan spirit, many will be called to join us so that we can go even to new areas.

With the care and help of Our Lady of Guadalupe and your enthusiasm and cooperation, we can make great things happen.

In Christ and Our Lady of Guadalupe,

Meldon

Father Meldon Hickey, O.F.M.
Minister Provincial

TEPEYAC. A former formation house of St. John the Baptist Province in Albuquerque, Tepeyac, named for the hill on which Our Lady of Guadalupe first appeared in Mexico, became the headquarters of the new province in the summer of 1985. (OLGPA.)

FIRST PROFESSION. The first friar to complete all of his initial formation in the new province, Michael Burns kneels to make his first profession of vows to Meldon Hickey at St. Michael Mission in 1987. (OLGPA.)

VOCATION DREAM FULFILLED. When Guadalupe Province was formed in 1985, the friars prayed for vocations from among the Navajo people. To date, Maynard Shurley, here vested by George Ward with the assistance of Bart Wolf (second from right), remains the only Navajo friar. (OLGPA.)

RICHARD ROHR. Moving from Cincinnati to Albuquerque with the idea of starting something new to proclaim the Gospel in a Franciscan way, in 1987, Richard founded the Center for Action and Contemplation. That ministry now reaches all around the world. Richard and his work have been featured in both popular and religious media. Nearly 300,000 people receive a daily e-mail taken from Richard's writings. (OLGPA.)

DIVERSITY. As this photograph from 2018 illustrates, even as Our Lady of Guadalupe Province has grown smaller, the background of the member friars has grown more diverse. Of 50 members of the province, not quite all here, only 2 have not been members or had significant formation experiences in other provinces, and all of the friars have in some way traversed cultural boundaries in their lives and ministries. (OLGPA.)

Seven

IT IS NOT OVER

Since 1985, when 100 friars of St. John the Baptist Province ministering in the Southwest were formed into the province of Our Lady of Guadalupe, friars have come to know the truth of John Vaughn's words, "Franciscan structures exist to serve the life and ministry of the friars. Friars do not exist to serve structures." At his urging, provinces went to work together in missions in Peru and Africa in the 1980s. In the 1990s, an interprovincial novitiate and post-novitiate program maintained the quality of initial formation, even as the quantity of friars available to conduct that formation shrank. Across province lines, friars began to look for ways to do things better together than they could do them alone.

In 2013, a commission of friars representing all seven provinces in the United States seriously studied the current reality of the friars of their provinces and their prospects for the future. They concluded that the status quo of seven provincial structures, often duplicating efforts, could not be sustained with the changing demographics of these friar communities. Further, for revitalization to occur, a critical mass of younger friars from all the provinces would need to come together. All the friars studied proposals for revitalization and restructuring their fraternal governance. In 2018, six provinces voted to deepen the process of revitalization by coming together into one new province that would stretch from coast to coast in an expression of confidence in God's help and the brightness of the future to come.

Trusted by Their Brothers. The leaders of the six provinces whose archives have contributed to this work history are, from left to right, James Gannon, David Gaa, Thomas Nairn, Jack Clark Robinson, Kevin Mullen, and Mark Soehner. They are engaged with their brothers in a deep effort to look toward the future with a deep faith that Franciscans have something special to offer the world and that the story begun in these pages is not over, but only begun. (OLGPA.)

HORSES? These final light photographs prove that Franciscans defy categorization, and in their adherence to what medieval Franciscan philosopher John Duns Scotus termed *haecceity*, or "this-ness," each is unique, even when that means they do not fit into the story an author is trying to tell. In the Franciscan rule, friars are forbidden to ride horses, but that does not mean they cannot admire them and the work that they do, as these friars of Sacred Heart Province in a picture from around the turn of the 20th century illustrate. (SHPA.)

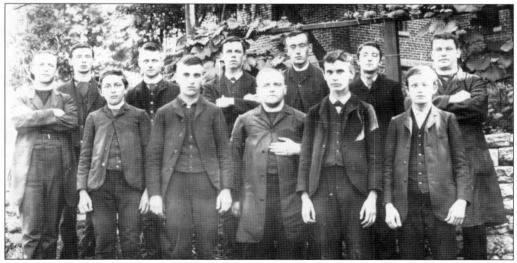

BRIGHT FUTURES. These high school seminarians of St. John the Baptist Province on an outing with their faculty in 1889, were dressed for success. The unassuming little fellow on the left in the front row, Albert Thomas Daeger, would 40 years later become archbishop of Santa Fe, New Mexico. (SJBPA.)

LOOK AT THE CAMERA. The largest single group of friars in a single photograph in this book is the provincial chapter of Holy Name Province in 2014. As in any photograph of this many friars, not everyone is looking at the camera nor has his eyes open, but they sure look like they enjoy being together. (HNPA.)

Merry Christmas! Serra Retreat, built in 1942, was the first retreat house of St. Barbara Province. This 1950s picture of the friars working at the retreat house is a vivid reminder that a retreat among Franciscans might be serious business but would never be solemn. (SBPA.)

FRANCISCANS AND ANIMALS. No compilation of photographs of Franciscan friars could be complete without some reference to animals. These cleric students of Assumption of the Blessed Virgin Mary Province in Green Bay, Wisconsin, in 1933 prove that even when taking their studies very seriously, Franciscans have time for their animal friends. (ABVMPA.)

Copyright 1906 by
Simeon Schwemberger

Guns and Ballots. Anselm Weber, by then the head of St. Michael Mission, the founding mission of Our Lady of Guadalupe Province, here casts his ballot in the Arizona Territorial election of 1906. The fellow with the six-shooter is no doubt there to see that Anselm does not try to vote twice and that rattlesnakes do not carry away the ballot box. (SJBPA.)

DISCOVER THOUSANDS OF LOCAL HISTORY BOOKS FEATURING MILLIONS OF VINTAGE IMAGES

Arcadia Publishing, the leading local history publisher in the United States, is committed to making history accessible and meaningful through publishing books that celebrate and preserve the heritage of America's people and places.

Find more books like this at
www.arcadiapublishing.com

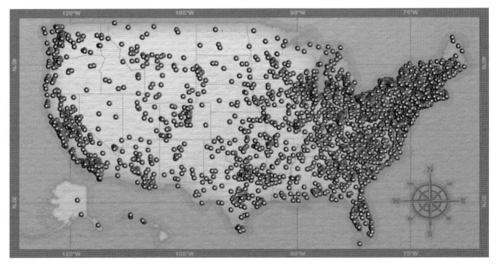

Search for your hometown history, your old stomping grounds, and even your favorite sports team.